CW01673657

OWEN JONES

THE ROMAN COURT

(INCLUDING THE ANTIQUE SCULPTURES IN THE NAVE)

ERECTED IN THE

CRYSTAL PALACE

DESCRIBED BY GEORGE SCHARF

Elibron Classics
www.elibron.com

Elibron Classics series.

ISBN 1-4021-7071-8 (paperback)
ISBN 1-4021-0192-9 (hardcover)

This Elibron Classics Replica Edition is an unabridged facsimile of the edition published in 1854 by Crystal Palace Library; and by Bradbury & Evans, London.

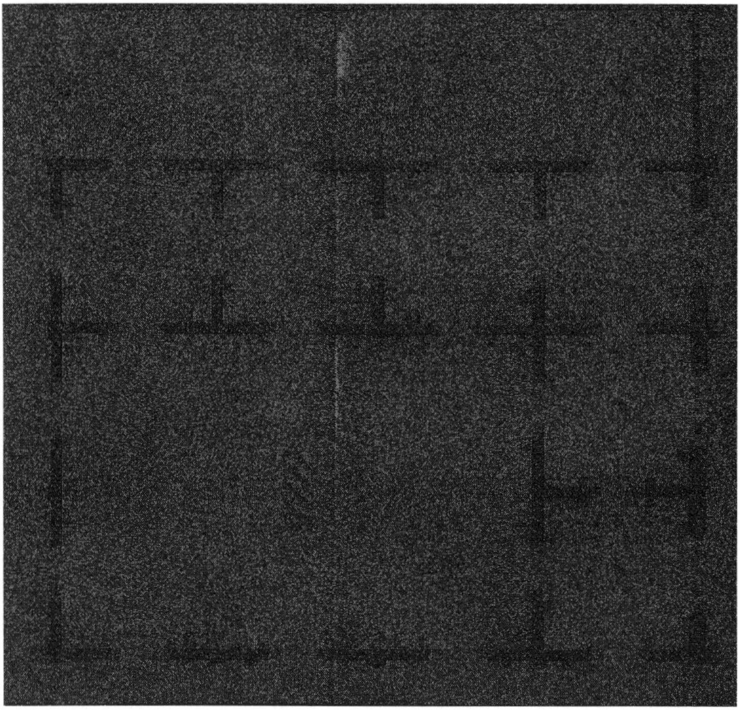

THE

ROMAN COURT

(INCLUDING THE ANTIQUE SCULPTURES IN THE NAVE)

ERECTED IN THE

CRYSTAL PALACE,

BY OWEN JONES.

DESCRIBED BY GEORGE SCHARF, JUN.

F.S.A., F.R.S.L., &c.

CRYSTAL PALACE LIBRARY;

AND

BRADBURY & EVANS, 11, BOUVERIE STREET, LONDON.

1854.

BRADBURY AND EVANS,
PRINTERS TO THE CRYSTAL PALACE COMPANY,
WHITEFRIARS.

PREFACE TO ROMAN COURT.

THE arts practised and elaborated amongst the Romans, owed their origin to the inspiration of the genius of the Greek, and served as a secondary development or continuation of his wonderful achievements. On that account this little book can only be regarded as an extension of the Greek Court Catalogue. I have therefore but to refer the reader of prefaces to the preliminary observations appended to that work. I anxiously hope that friends will make every allowance for the unavoidable haste with which the following pages have been prepared, and that they will favour me with their suggestions and corrections in time for the second edition. In quotation, I have availed myself of the vigorous language of Sir Thomas North, and the learned Philemon Holland. The friends named in my preface to the Greek Court Catalogue have rendered me equal assistance with regard to the sculptures in this department. I therefore take this opportunity of repeating my cordial gratitude to them.

1, TORRINGTON SQUARE,
May 27th.

CONTENTS.

PAGE

ARCHITECTURE OF THE ROMAN COURT 3

HISTORY OF THE PROGRESS OF ROMAN SCULPTURE 5

ETRUSCAN PERIOD 5

CONSTANTINOPOLITAN AGE 17

NOTES ON THE PRINCIPAL COLLECTIONS OF ANCIENT SCULPTURE IN EUROPE 19

THE VATICAN MUSEUM 20

THE CAPITOL MUSEUM 20

THE FARNESE COLLECTION 21

VILLA BORGHESE 21

VILLA ALBANI 21

VILLA LUDOVISI 21

VILLA MEDICI 21

PALAZZO SPADA 21

VILLA MONTALTO 22

MUSEO BORBONICO, NAPLES. 22

GALERIA IMPERIALE IN THE UFFIZII, FLORENCE 22

CAMPO SANTA, PISA . . . .

THE LOUVRE, PARIS 23

THE BRITISH MUSEUM, LONDON 24

THE ROYAL ACADEMY OF ARTS, LONDON 25

MUNICH 25

BERLIN 25

DRESDEN 26

VIENNA 26

MADRID 26

LIST OF THE PRINCIPAL ILLUSTRATED WORKS IN SCULPTURE . . 26

ROMAN COURT CATALOGUE 31

ÆGINA MARBLES 47

MONUMENT OF LYSICRATES 62

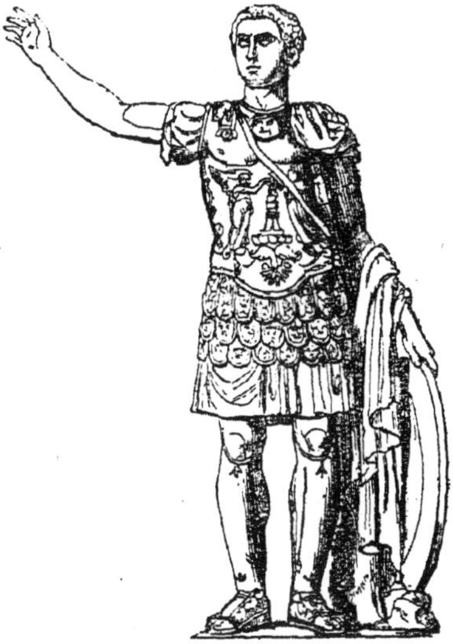

Statue of the Emperor Titus, from the Louvre.

THE ROMAN COURT.

ARCHITECTURE OF ROMAN COURT.

The Roman Court externally to the nave presents three arches of the Tuscan order, which is the earliest style of columnar architecture found in Italy. This façade is taken from the lowest range of columns on the outside of the Coliseum at Rome. The arch, as a decoration to buildings, has until very lately been regarded as peculiar to the Romans; nevertheless it was long known to the Egyptians, and consequently to the Greeks, but not used by them for any external purposes. In Assyria, on the other hand, the most recent discoveries prove that it was not only employed for vaulting and underground support, but that at

Nineveh it was used as a grand architectural feature, and a powerful means of producing combinations with other forms.

Among all the architectural designs of the ancient Greeks, seen so abundantly in their small tombs, stelæ, and cippi, the arch—even as a mere form—is avoided. They seem always to have preferred the triangular, pedimental form, or the fleuron (woodcut, No. 149, page 87 of Greek Court) as a heading. In very few instances of a late period, judging from the style of art, and the inscription in Greek characters, is the arch form to be seen. These examples are in the British Museum and the Louvre (see woodcut, where a niche containing figures appears upon the flat surface of the usual formed cippus). These works are probably of the period of the Antonines, when Roman fashion predominated, and they accord with a figure in a niche at the back of the theatre at Myra in Lycia, where the Greek inscription also marks a Roman age. Large niches and surfaces decorated with square, diagonal, and circular lines seem to have been the predominant characteristics of the ancient Roman decoration for internal walls. The existing paintings of the baths of Titus and Livia, at Rome, lead to this conclusion. Their ceilings were divided into numerous little compartments of this kind, and not unfrequently niches were painted with rich flutings in the upper part, like the ribbing of a shell, with the hinge uppermost.

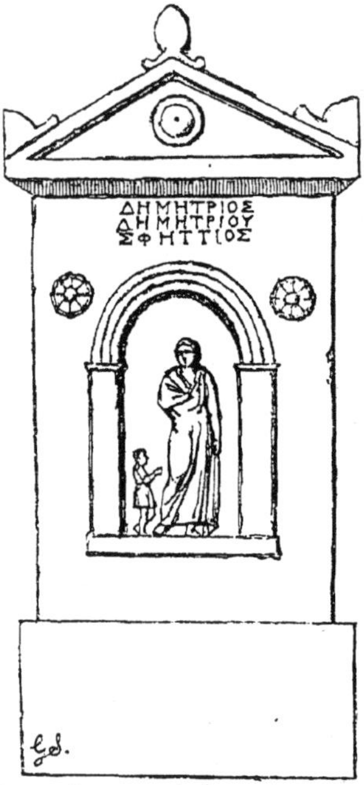

Greek Cippus, with an arch introduced in it, from the Louvre.

The profuse extent to which the Romans employed precious marbles has led very materially to the decoration of the interior of this court, and the rarest marbles have been accordingly imitated upon the walls.

The ceilings of the corridors, which open upon the long gallery, have been painted and decorated in accordance with remaining examples at Rome. Although at this time, the ceilings of the imperial baths in that city are almost obliterated, careful engravings and copies were made from them, and we possess in the designs of Raphael, and the arabesques of Giovanni da Udine and Giulio Romano, studies and transcripts of some of their finest compositions.

INTRODUCTORY OUTLINE OF THE PROGRESS OF ROMAN SCULPTURE, TAKEN FROM ANCIENT AUTHORS, AND ILLUSTRATED BY EXAMPLES IN THE VARIOUS MUSEUMS OF EUROPE.

THE Romans were not originally an art-loving people. They began by conquest, and at once employed the talents of those whom they subdued. By the assistance of their neighbours the Etruscans, they overcame other neighbouring tribes, and erected great public works in their city. Vastness of size characterised these productions. The arch which the Etruscans had brought with them from Asia Minor, derived thither from Assyria, was employed as the most powerful principle of support, and the whole city was undermined by drains, arched over with cuneiform stones. The Etruscans seem to have been an industrious people; they cultivated the arts, and carried on extensive commerce even whilst the Roman state was struggling into existence.

ETRUSCAN PERIOD, 510—167, B.C.

B.C. 510. EXPULSION OF THE TARQUINS FROM ROME, AND THE PISISTRATIDÆ FROM ATHENS. DARIUS HYSTASPES KING OF PERSIA AND OF EGYPT ALSO.

The Romans did nothing for themselves. In their earlier days they depended upon the Etruscans for all refinements of art, in the same way as at a later period they depended upon the Greeks, and accordingly, when workmen were required for any purpose, they were sent for from Etruria.

The Tuscans prepared baked clay, or terra-cotta, figures for the great temple of Jupiter Capitolinus, and when finished, sent them to Rome. Their style of architecture was peculiar; it was an offshoot from the Doric. This also was soon introduced into Rome. The early statues which decorated the city were remarkable for their magnitude. Many were wrought in clay, and others in bronze; but wood seems to have been rarely used amongst them. Carvilius made a bronze colossus of Jupiter from the armour taken in the Samnite war, so vast, that as it stood on the capitol, it was distinctly visible from the Jupiter Latiaris on the Alban Mount.* One of the annual ceremonies at Rome consisted in fresh painting the statue of Jupiter in the capitol with

* It was so large that a complete statue of Carvilius himself was made out of the mere filings of the metal, which was placed at the foot of the other.

bright vermilion. An early metal work of the Etruscan period is the celebrated Wolf of the capitol, given in the frontispiece of this catalogue. The boys are modern, but the wolf is executed in all the rigidity and elaboration peculiar to early art.

Pliny mentions a superb Etruscan colossus of bronze, fifty feet high, representing Apollo, placed in the Palatine library belonging to the temple of Augustus. However wonderful the size, he says, nothing can compare with the beauty of the figure, or the workmanship of the metal.

A bronze statue of a Chimæra, and a life-sized portrait of an orator in the toga, with an inscription on the border, display great proficiency in the art of metal casting: these two last-mentioned statues still exist at Florence. Another class of art peculiar to the Etruscans was the engraving of various figures and devices in pure outline upon smooth pieces of bronze, which were used for mirrors and mirror cases, or to adorn metal boxes containing various articles of the toilet. It has always been a matter of surprise that this process did not lead earlier to the art of printing. The ancients had their wooden stamps and stencillings, as we see by Assyria and Pompeii, a still closer approximation to our modern practices, and yet they never seem to have advanced beyond the multiplication of seals and coins. In the time of the Republic, the Romans devoted especial attention to military works, road-making, and aqueducts often extending many miles upon a series of arches. Few monuments of the republican period still remain. One distinguished Roman, the founder of the Fabian house, cultivated painting, and adorned the temple of Salus (Health), at Rome, with his works, B.C. 304. Hence he received the name of Fabius Pictor. We read also of numerous statues to great men being erected in the forum and other places; and the custom of elevating statues upon columns seems peculiar to the Romans. The sarcophagus of Scipio, now in the Vatican, exhibits all the strength of Tuscan influence. The early Roman coins are especially bad, and those of the various families preserved in the cabinets of collectors are clumsy imitations of Greek types; but they belong to a very recent period of the republic. The year 275 B.C. is remarkable, as it witnessed the first Roman triumph over a Grecian army. Pyrrhus, king of Epirus, crossed to Italy in defence of the people of Tarentum, but was driven back by the Romans; and the war terminated in the most brilliant triumph Rome had then achieved. These successes, together with the subjugation of Sicily, and the prosperous progress of the war with Carthage, determined the Romans to carry their arms into Greece itself. War commenced accordingly, and in the year 168 B.C. Paulus Æmilius sent Metellus to Rome to announce the overthrow of Perseus, king of Macedonia, at the battle of Pydna.

GRECIAN INFLUENCE.

B.C. 167. CONQUEST OF MACEDON. PERSEUS LED CAPTIVE THROUGH ROME, ANTIOCHUS KING OF SYRIA, PHARNACES OF PONTUS, EUMENES OF PERGAMUS, PTOLEMY OF EGYPT. ENNIUS AND TERENCE FLOURISH IN LITERATURE.

The triumph of Paulus Æmilius the following year is minutely recorded by Plutarch, and affords the first instance of those magnificent spectacles for which Rome became afterwards so celebrated. Every variety of foreign production that could be brought by way of plunder was displayed; costly armour, vases, and precious metals, delighted the gazing multitude; and the captives, with their families, added to the dreadful reality of the scene. Even Perseus himself walked before the chariot of the conqueror. Paintings and statues of enormous size, mounted upon platforms, were drawn along upon 250 chariots. Plutarch's description of the triumph of Æmilius, in the words of his quaint translator Sir Thomas North, gives too complete a picture to be omitted:

"First, the people having set up sundry scaffolds as well in the lists and field called Circos by the Latins, where the games and common running of horses and chariots are made, as also about the market-place, and in other streets of the city, which the shew of the triumph should pass; they all presented themselves in their best gowns to see the magnificence and state thereof. All the temples of the gods also were set wide open, hanged full of garlands and flowers, and all perfumed within; and there were set through all the quarters of the city, numbers of sergeants and other officers holding tipstaves in their hands to order the stragling people, and to keep them up in corners and lane-ends that they should not pester the streets and hinder the triumph. Furthermore, the sight of this triumph was to continue three days, wherof the first was scant sufficient to see the passing-by of the images, tables and pictures, and statues of wonderful bigness, all won and gotten of their enemies, and drawn in the shew upon 250 chariots. The second day, there was carried upon a number of carts, all the fairest and richest armour of the Macedonians, as well of copper as also of iron and steel, all glistering bright, being newly furbished, and artificially laid in order (and yet in such sort as if they had been cast in heaps, one upon another, without taking any care otherwise for the ordering and laying of them), fair burganets upon targets; habergions, or brigantines and corslets, upon greaves; round targets of the Cretans, and javelins of the Thracians, and arrows amongst the armed pikes ; all this armour and carriage being bound one to another so trimly (neither being too loose nor too straight) that one hitting against another as they drew them upon the carts through the city, they made such a sound and noise as it was fearful to hear it : so that the only sight of these spoils of the captives being overcome made the sight so much more terrible to behold. After these carts, laden with armour, there followed 3000 men which carried the ready money in 750 vessels, which weighed about three talents a-piece, and every one of them were carried by four men ; and there were other that carried great bowls of silver, cups and goblets fashioned like pitchers, and other pots to drink in, goodly to behold, as well for their bigness, as for their great and singular imbossed works about them. The third day, early in the morning, the trumpets began to sound and set forwards, sounding no march, nor sweet note to beautifie the triumph withall ; but they blew out the brave alarum they sound at an assault to give the soldiers courage for to fight. After them followed sixscore goodly fat oxen, having all their horns gilt, and garlands of flowers and nosegays about their heads, and there went by them certain young men, with aprons of needlework, girt about their middle, who led them to the sacrifice, and young boys with them also, that carried goodly basons of gold and silver, to cast and sprinkle the blood of the sacrifices about. And after these followed those that carried all coins of gold, devided by basons and vessels, and every one of them weighing three talents as they did before, that carried the great holy cup which Emylius had caused to be made of massive gold, set full of precious stones, weighing the weight of ten talents, to make an offering unto the gods. And next unto them went other that carried plate made and wrought after antique fashion, and notable cups of the ancient kings of Macedon ; as the cup called Antigonus, and another Seleucus ; and to be short all the whole cupboard of plate of gold and silver of King Perseus. And next them came the chariot of his armour, in the which was all King Perseus' harness, and his royal band (they call a Diadem) upon his armour. And a little space between them followed next the king's children, whom they led prisoners, with the train of their schoolmasters and other officers, and their servants weeping and lamenting; who held up their hands unto the people that looked upon them and taught the king's young children to do the like, to ask mercy and grace at the people's hands. There were three pretty little children—two sons and a daughter—amongst them, whose tender years and lack of understanding made them (poor souls) they could not feel their present misery, which made the people so much the more to pity them, when they saw the poor little infants that knew not the change of their fortune; so that for the compassion they had of them, they allmost let the father pass without looking upon him. Many people's hearts did melt for very pity, that the tears ran down their cheeks, so as this sight brought both pleasure and sorrow, together, to the lookers-on, until they were past and gone a good way out of sight. King Perseus the father followed after his children and their train, and he was clothed in a black gown, wearing a pair of slippers on his feet, after his country manner. He shewed by his countenance his troubled mind, oppressed with sorrow of his most miserable state and fortune: he was followed with his kinsfolks, his familiar friends, his officers and houshold servants, their faces disfigured by blubering, shewing to the world by their lamenting tears and sorrowfull eyes cast upon their unfortunate master, how much they sorrowed and bewailed his most hard and cruel fortune, little accounting of their own misery. The voice goeth that Perseus sent unto Æmylius to entreat him that he should not be led through the city in the shew and sight of the triumph. But Æmylius mocking (as he deserved) his cowardly faint heart, answered: As for that, it was before, and is now in him to do if he will. Meaning to let him understand thereby, that he might rather choose to die, than living to receive such open shame. Howbeit his heart would not serve him, he was so cowardly and made so effeminate by a certain vain hope, he knew not what, that he was contented to make one among his own spoils. After all this there followed 400 princely crowns of gold which the cities and towns of Greece had purposely sent by their ambassadors unto Æmylius, to honour his victory; and next he came himself in his chariot triumphing, which was passing sumptuously set forth and adorned. It was a noble sight to behold, and yet the person of himself only was worth the looking on, without all that great pomp and magnificence. For he was apparelled in a purple gown branched with gold, and carried in his right hand a laurell-bough, as all his army did besides; the which being divided by bands and companies, followed the triumphing chariot of their captain, some of the soldiers singing songs of victory which the Romans use to sing in like triumphs, mingling them with merry, pleasant toyes, rejoicing at their captain; other of them also did sing songs of triumph, in the honour and praise of Æmylius' noble conquest and victory. He was openly praised, blessed, and honoured of everybody, and neither hated nor envied of honest men."

Æmilius himself is said to have been a great admirer of the fine arts; he paid an express visit to the statue of Jupiter, by Phidias, at Olympia; but where Perseus had intended to dedicate a golden statue at Delphi, the conqueror ordered his own image to be set up instead.

Another triumph, that of Metellus, 146 B.C., was still further connected with Greek art. He had, in order to give effect to his procession, brought over the group of Alexander and the horsemen who fell at the battle of the Granicus, by Lysippus. This is the first record of any particular work of Grecian fame being introduced into Rome.

Mummius completed the conquest of Greece, 146 B.C., the same year that Carthage was razed to the ground. The Carthaginians themselves had formerly plundered the maritime towns of Sicily, and the Persians and Macedonians had, in their victories, carried off all works of art as a lawful prize of conquest; so that the Romans did not act without precedent. Mummius, it is said, plundered more works of art than all his predecessors put together. He destroyed many works through ignorance of their value; and his soldiers were seen playing at dice upon one of the celebrated pictures of Aristides.

When Pompey triumphed over Mithridates, the chief attraction was the display of engraved gems, pearls, and golden statues. These new luxuries of the Romans are noticed also by Pliny (His. Nat. Bk. 37, ch. i.); he says—

"Cæsar, when Dictator, consecrated, in the Temple of Venus Genitrix, six cabinets or caskets of rings and jewels; and Marcellus, son to Octavia, dedicated one in the Temple Palatine of Apollo. Finally, this is to be observed, that the said victorie of Pompeius, which he atchieved over K. Mithridates, set men's teeth at Rome a watering after pearls and precious stones; like as the conquest obtained by L. Scipio and Cn. Manlius brought them into love with silver plate curiously enchased and embossed: also with rich hanging of cloth of gold, silver, and tissue; together with beds and tables of brass; even as the brasen statues and vessels of Corinthian brass, and the curious painted tables, came in request upon the victory that L. Mummius gained over Achæa.

"To the end that it may appear more evidently what the triumph of Pompey wrought in this respect, I will put down, word for word, what I find upon record in the registers that bear witness of the actes which passed during those triumphs. In the third triumph, therefore, which was decreed unto him (for that he had scoured the seas of pirates and rovers, reduced Natolia, and the kingdom of Pontus, under the dominion of the Romans, defeated kings and nations, according as I have declared in the seventh book of my history), he entered Rome the last day of September, in the year when M. Piso and M. Messala were Consuls, on which day there was carried before him, in shew, a chess-board with all the men, and the same board was made of two precious stones, and yet it was two foot broad and four foot long; and lest any man should doubt hereof, and think it incredible, considering that no gems at this day come near thereto in bigness, know he, that in this triumph, he shewed a golden moon weighing thirty pounds; three dining tables, also of gold; other vessel, likewise of massive gold and precious stones, as much as would garnish nine cupboards; three images of beaten gold, representing Minerva, Mars, and Apollo; coronets made of stones, to the number of three-and-thirty; a mountain made of gold four square, wherin a man might see red deer, lions, fruit-trees of all sorts, and the whole mountain environed and compassed all about with a vine of gold; moreover, an oratory or closet consisting of pearl, in the top or louver whereof there was a clock or horologe. He caused also to be borne before him, in a pompous shew, his own image, made of pearls; the portraiture (I say) of that Cn. Pompeius, whom regal majesty and ornaments would have better beseemed; and that good face and venerable visage so highly honoured among all nations, was now all of pearls; as if that manly countenance and severity of his had been vanquished, and riotous excess and superfluity had triumphed over him, rather than he over it.

* * * * * * *

"This victory of his brought into Rome, first our cups, and other vessels of Cassidoine; and Pompey himself was the first who, that very day of his triumph, presented unto Jupiter Capitolinus six such cups; and presently, from that time forward, men also began to have a mind unto them in cupboards, counting tables, yea, and in vessel for the kitchen, and to serve up meat in."

Sylla committed heartless and systematic depredations at Athens and Olympia, and his soldiers were permitted to ravage to any extent. Verres also, when governor of Sicily, was accused of plundering the island of its finest works of art; he had previously devastated Achaia, Pontus, and other parts of Asia Minor in the same manner.

Augustan Age.

B.C. 30. CONQUEST OF EGYPT. DEATH OF ANTONY AND CLEOPATRA. HORACE, VIRGIL, AND LIVY FLOURISH IN LITERATURE.

When Octavius won the victory at Actium, he enlarged the temple of Apollo upon that promontory, and expressed his gratitude by dedicating the statue of Apollo, by Scopas, in a temple at Rome, on the Palatine hill. Augustus declared that he had found Rome of brick, and would leave it of marble. At first the Romans seem to have contented themselves with good copies of the celebrated sculptures in Greece, and therefore we may assign to this period many of the fine works which are still extant. Such copies must have been multiplied extensively, in order to gratify various tastes; but they are rarely exactly alike—differences between them, easily seen on comparison, occur, as in the Apollo Sauroctonos, Nos. 298 and 301, and the Jason, Nos. 21 and 25. There seems even to have been some scruple with regard to direct imitation. That they did closely imitate is proved, however, by the singular circumstance that in many instances several repetitions of the same statue have been found *together*. As many as four in the same place of the Boy and Goose, No. 269, and three of the Boy and Bird, No. 263. The Laocoon also was found in close connection with a second group greatly mutilated; and in the villa of Hadrian several figures were discovered under similar circumstances. Much occupation was given in the Augustan age to statuaries by portraiture, and to this period we owe some of the finest examples of statesmen in that most noble of all dresses, the *Toga*. The *Toga* was originally derived from the Tuscans, but it appears to have become more amplified in course of time; for, although clearly recognisable on Etruscan monuments, it is by no means so full, and differs little from the pallium of the Greeks, beyond the mode of adjustment. Portrait statues of Augustus and Tiberius in the toga are particularly fine. Numerous basreliefs representing religious ceremonies and sacrifices are of good workmanship, and accord with the coins of the period. The worship of Isis, introduced at the beginning of the Empire, brought with it strange tastes, and led to peculiar varieties of dress and manners. Nero threw down the statues of victors in Greece out of envy, and further evinced his bad taste by gilding a statue of Alexander, by Lysippus. He displayed his extravagance in his Golden House, for which from Delphi alone he brought 500 statues; and his vanity may be estimated by his having had his portrait painted 120 feet high. Buildings crowded more

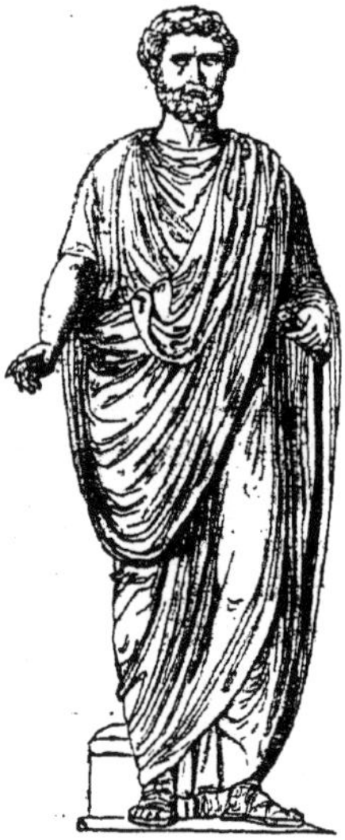

Statue of Didius Julianus, from the Louvre, showing the Toga.

and more round the Palatine hill ; and pile was raised upon pile with no other object than to gratify the builder and minister to the grossest licentiousness. Works of a more public utility were constructed by the Flavii. The amphitheatre called the Coliseum was founded by Vespasian, A.D. 72, and completed by Titus eight years later. Calculated to hold 87,000 spectators, it was chiefly built by the Jewish exiles. Externally it presented the form of an ellipse, decorated with four ranges of arches, one above the other.

The baths of Titus, many portions of which still exist, afford us sufficient examples of the taste of the day in pictorial decoration. The ceilings aud walls of the apartments are covered with the lightest and most beautiful paintings, similar in style to those found at Pompeii and Herculaneum, cities that were overwhelmed in this reign. A great part of the baths of Titus occupied the site of the Golden House of Nero, which was originally built upon the house and gardens of Mæcenas. Nero, it seems, embodied the villa of Mæcenas in his design, and these were again made use of by Titus ; so that we probably behold in these decorations some of the very images which were devised by the patron of Horace and the friend of Augustus. In these chambers were found the Pluto and Cerberus, and the Meleager of the Vatican, also the celebrated painting called the Nozze Aldobrandini. The famous group of the Laocoon, found in the neighbourhood of the baths of Titus, and supposed to have been executed in this reign, is minutely described by Pliny.

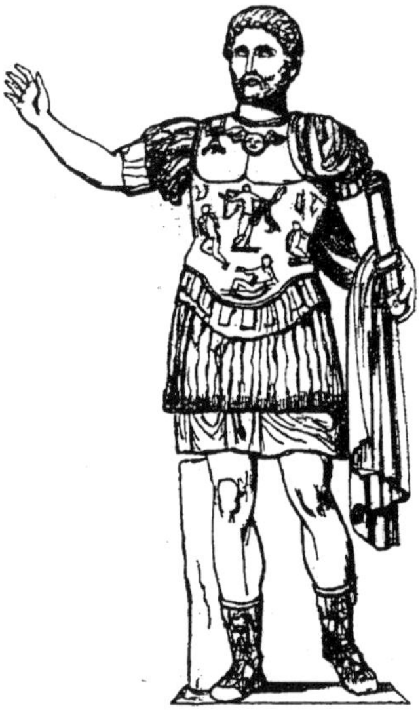

Statue of Hadrian from the British Museum.

Trajan indulged a passion for architecture, and, with the assistance of Apollodorus, erected many splendid buildings in Rome. His own forum was the most famous of all. Some very rich ornamental pieces of architecture, Nos. 96 and 98, belong to this period. Hadrian, who pretended to a knowledge and practice of architecture, put Apollodorus to death because he had criticized the emperor's works too boldly. The age of Hadrian was notwithstanding a flourishing period for art. Every possible excellence as regards execution seems to have been revived ; but still the creative power of invention was wanting. How superlatively excellent the technical art was in these days may be seen by the many figures of Antinous. This favourite of the emperor seems to have been represented in almost every variety of size, character, and material. The most beautiful examples are the Capitol and Farnese statues, Nos. 280 and 288, and the Albani basrelief, No. 143. Copying any of the finest Greek statues, with such powers of workmanship, the sculptors might well produce specimens not to be distinguished from the originals. Hadrian erected a villa at Tibur — the modern Tivoli—where he designed to include in one spot all the most striking objects noted in his travels. It contained a Lyceum, an Academy, a Pœcile, in imitation of that at Athens, a Vale of Tempe, Serapeon of Canopus, a Library, a Tartarus, Elysian fields, and numerous temples and theatres. Here were deposited numberless statues, many of them copies or recollections of foreign works, mosaics, and costly vases of every description. During his reign, Hadrian had visited the principal parts of his vast empire, conferring benefits wherever he went, and in almost every instance leaving some monument of his generosity behind him. His numerous medals show his progresses :—each grateful place or city being represented upon a distinct coin as a female figure welcoming him. When a town was rebuilt, or a province colonized anew, it was represented as a prostrate female, and the emperor raising her by the hand.

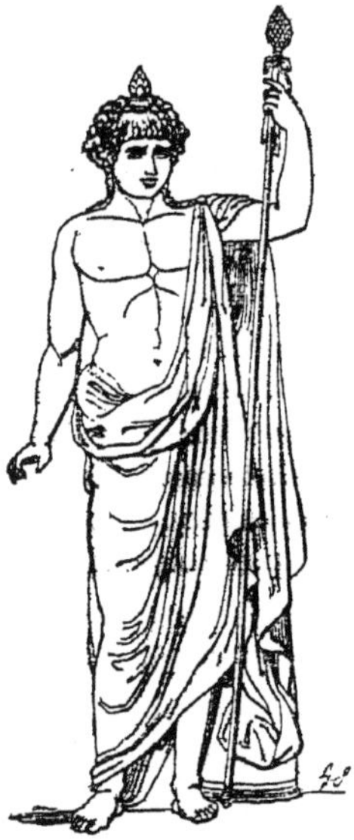

Colossal statue of Antinous, formerly in the Braschi Palace, now in the Lateran Museum at Rome. See No. 347 of the Catalogue.

The temple of Jupiter Olympius at Athens was crowded with bronze statues of the emperor Hadrian, each having been contributed by one of the cities that had received benefits from him. They were placed in front of the columns. The enclosure surrounding the temple, to the extent of more than half a mile, was also full of statues. This fulsome repetition of one personage did not originate with the age of Hadrian. Demetrius Phalereus was honoured by the Athenians with 360 statues, and yet before the same number of days had elapsed they were all broken to pieces. The people of Rome ordered a statue of Marius Gratidianus to be erected in *every street*, and these were overthrown upon the approach of Sylla. Pausanias says that Hadrian dedicated the temple of Jupiter Olympius with an ivory and gold statue of the deity, not inferior in size to a Roman or Rhodian colossus. The Athenians surpassed the votive statues of all other cities in a colossus of the emperor, which was placed between the Temple and the Parthenon. Hadrian also built a temple of Juno and of Jupiter Panhellenius ; one of his edifices at Athens was supported by 120 pillars of Phrygian marble, with a portico of the same, and ceilings of alabaster enriched with gold. The side walls were adorned with pictures and statues. He also gave the Athenians a library and gymnasium supported by 100 columns of Libyan marble, which bore his name.

In these works he seems to have emulated the liberality of a private individual named Herodes, a native of Athens, who lived in the reign of the emperor Nerva. This Herodes Atticus became suddenly rich by the discovery of vast treasure, and his chief gratification was to enrich the city of his birth with public buildings and useful works.

Hadrian constructed his own monument—now the castle of St. Angelo—at Rome, and his remains were conveyed to it from the neighbourhood of Baiæ, where he died. The tomb was most probably finished by his successor, Antoninus Pius. It was built of Parian marble, adorned with statues of men and horses, and rose high above the walls of the city. When, in subsequent times, the Goths besieged the city, the statues were torn down from their pedestals and hurled upon the assailants. Many valuable fragments have been discovered at the foot of this structure, among them the famous Barberini Faun, No. 19. The age of the Antonines was also favourable to art, and the series of medals struck in their time exhibits the finest examples of mythic illustrations and historical events of any known period. The coins of Greece struck during the Roman empire are extremely interesting for the subjects they represent—frequently, celebrated statues, and sometimes buildings ; but the style of art is so coarse and inferior that only a general idea of what is intended can be obtained. Cameos, in the early period of the Roman empire, were wrought extensively, and some of the best portraits have been preserved in this manner. Particularly fine specimens are extant in the collections at Paris and Vienna. Cameos and gems are less satisfactory as evidences of the progress of art, because they were mostly done to gratify private caprice or some particular taste. Coins, on the other hand, were the affair of the state, and regarded also in a religious light.

A fine sculpture of the time of the Antonines is in the Louvre, representing Achilles among the daughters of Lycomedes. It is probably in itself a copy from a still better work, but an inferior repetition now at Rome affords the connoisseur an opportunity of judging how the same subject borne down the stream of time loses in spirit, and in the original intention. The Roman copy is the celebrated sarcophagus of the capitol in which the Portland vase was discovered. A cast of this sarcophagus is now in the British Museum.

Fashion, especially in arranging the hair, occupied much of the attention of the Roman ladies. Romans were frequently represented as Greek divinities, and denuded accordingly, but the hair, a never failing distinction, was allowed to remain in the fashion of the day, however extravagant it might be. Julia, the daughter of the Emperor Titus, figures thus as a statue of Venus. Noble Romans and their wives are immortalized as Venus and Mars, some as Juno, and not a few fond mothers and ugly children are perpetuated as Venus and Cupid.

In ornamented sarcophagi of late times, the multitude of subjects corresponds with the overloaded images in Latin poetry. Exuberant architectural ornament answers to a profusion of words, and after the period of Commodus, the sculptor seems to have worked merely from that which had been done by his predecessor, without the least regard to the fountain of all truth—*nature*. Even in the triumphal arches of Septimius Severus, the figures are deficient in life; they are only interesting to the antiquary as minute copies of armour, costume, and military engines. The ideal figures, such as the River gods in the spandrils of the arches, and Victories on the pedestals, are miserably bad. The features are exaggerated, and the outer folds of the drapery strongly marked, without any regard to the moulding of the limbs upon which they ought to rest. In sarcophagi, when the forms are so closely crowded, we often find small figures placed at the feet of larger ones, nay, in the very front of them, and every opening is filled with some secondary device either of figures or emblems. Architectural ornament gradually superseded the human figure, and we find large niches and fluted columns, dividing the figures even where a connection seems to be intended.

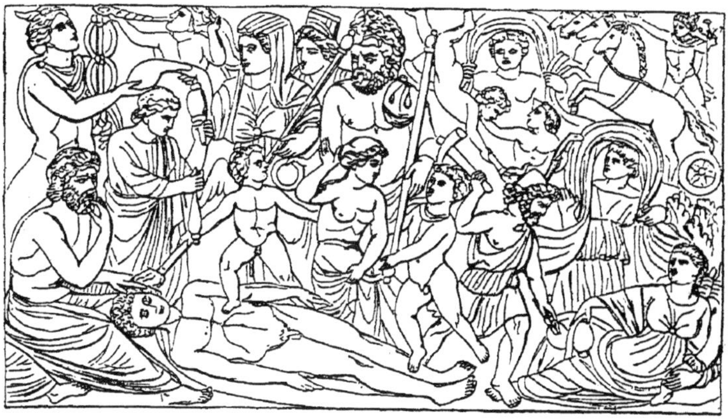

Portion of a Sarcophagus at Naples, representing Prometheus making images of man. Cupid animates the figures with his torch. Mercury, the Fates, Jupiter, Juno, Apollo, Aurora, and the Earth, occupy the background. Specimen of late Grecian art, under Roman influence.

The coins of the late period mark the same decline. Even portraiture upon them loses its force, and the artist seems to have depended more upon the name inscribed, and the ornaments of dress, and emblems, for recognition, than upon any particular character in the features. In many of the coins of this period of the empire we find the dresses and insignia most carefully elaborated, and therefore for purposes of costume, they are invaluable.

The arch of Constantine at Rome, to commemorate his victory over Maxentius, is only the reconstruction of a former arch, built in honour of Trajan. The greater part of the basreliefs refer to the actions of Trajan, and a few figures of Victory, and a frieze showing the conquest of Verona and the fall of Maxentius are all that belong to Constantine's own time. These sculptures are wretched in the extreme, and contrast sadly with the Trajan basreliefs, which are so excellent that Raphael has taken some of his finest compositions from them.

Constantinopolitan Age.

A.D. 330. REMOVAL FROM ROME TO CONSTANTINOPLE, DESTRUCTION OF THE HEATHEN TEMPLES, THEODOSIUS THE GREAT, EMPEROR OF ROME.

When the seat of the empire was removed to Constantinople, few artists remained, and all the finest works went thither also. The most celebrated statues that had been brought over from Greece, both in bronze and marble, were required to decorate the palaces of the Emperor and his nobility. Much may have perished on the way, but in the wars that ensued during the decline of the empire, all taste or regard for art seems to have been abandoned. The barbarians, during their inroads for plunder, sought only for precious material, bronze and silver statues rarely escaped, but marble works were broken into pieces, or used as mere building material. Statues were often coined into money. When Constantinople was taken by the Latins at the beginning of the 13th century, A.D. 1204, the remains of art appear to have suffered the greatest destruction; Nicetas, an eye-witness, describes the ruthless outrage and wanton destruction of every work of refinement. He records the glorious works of Polycletus, Lysippus, and other great sculptors as perishing on that occasion, but repeated conflagrations in the imperial palaces

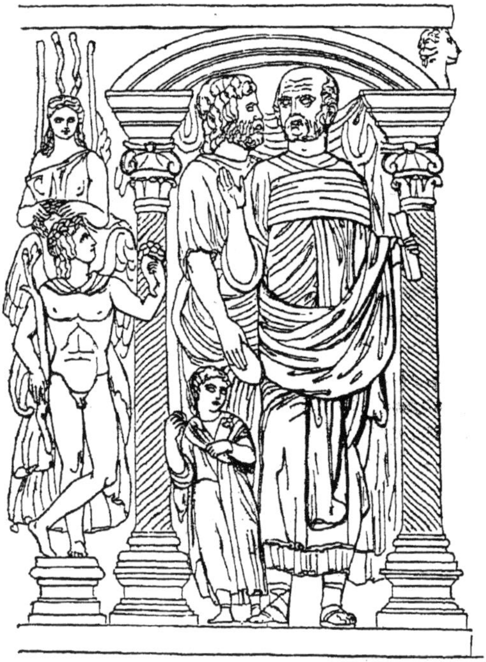

Bas-relief of late Roman times, from the Vatican.

had already lessened the number of illustrious works. Even the

Venus of Cnidos, and the ivory statues of Phidias, which had not been allowed to remain on the spot where they had so long been worshipped, perished at Constantinople before the calamities recorded by Nicetas took place. The four bronze horses now at Venice were saved from this destruction. They had been brought from Corinth, and are now attributed, but with little authority, to Lysippus. They are certainly far inferior to the masterpieces of Greece, and do not resemble the horses of that country in general appearance. From this period all collections and encouragement of art seem to have ceased. It was not till after Constantinople was captured by the Turks in the 15th century, when the remaining Greek families were expelled, that a taste for ancient literature arose in the West. These fugitive Greeks carried with them the taste for the ancient Greek language. Ancient manuscripts were sought for in Italy, and relics of statues supposed to illustrate them carefully treasured. From this age—the age when printing was first introduced—art was recognized. Wealthy individuals formed private galleries which were assiduously frequented by a privileged few. Collections of pictures and statues then became necessary adjuncts to the palaces of enlightened rulers. Now they are not only recognized as a means of public instruction, but enjoyed as a very considerable source of popular recreation.

NOTES ON THE PRINCIPAL COLLECTIONS OF ANCIENT SCULPTURE IN EUROPE.

When the Florentine, Poggio Bracciolini, wrote in 1430, he described six statues as all that remained then visible in Rome. He was Apostolic secretary to Pope Martin V., and busied himself especially in collecting ancient MSS., and making records of antiquarian subjects.

The six statues consisted of the *two* colossi, with their horses now on Monte Cavallo, *two* recumbent statues representing the Nile and Tiber, the *fifth* a reclining colossal figure of Ocean, known by the name of Marforio, removed by Sixtus V. to the Capitol (Bunsen, vol. iii., p. 138); the *sixth*, the famous bronze gilt statue of Marcus Aurelius on horseback, which stood at that time near the Lateran palace.

These were all the statues then to be seen in Rome, nor had any one begun to form collections of antiquities in that city, but Bracciolini had himself amassed many curiosities in his own country, and even sent to Rhodes in order to obtain sculptures of genuine Greek origin; his collection included choice intaglios, gems, and antique coins. Inspired by his enthusiasm, Cosmo di Medici began to form a museum at Florence, which increased afterwards under the auspices of Lorenzo into the far-famed Museum Florentinum.

THE VATICAN MUSEUM

Was founded by Julius II. It is the finest collection of statues in the world. Julius employed the famous Bramante to erect a vast niche surmounted by a gallery called Belvedere, and in front of this he collected in a garden the choicest statues extant in his day. These were the Nile and Tiber already described, a sarcophagus with the fable of Meleager, the famous Torso of Hercules (No. 67), and the celebrated group of Laocoon, which was kept in a separate alcove. To these his successor, Leo X., added the famous statue of the Mercury (No. 316), and the Apollo. The reclining Ariadne at that time adorned a fountain in the adjacent corridor.

Towards the end of the last century, Clement XIV. (Ganganelli), and Pius VI. (Braschi), formed the magnificent galleries in the Vatican, which bear their conjoined names in the Museo Pio Clementino. Many purchases were made from the collection of the Villa Negroni, previously Montalto, formed by Sixtus V., and from a series of excavations carried on among the ruins of Hadrian's Villa and elsewhere, by an energetic Scotchman named Gavin Hamilton. At the treaty of Tolentino in 1797 all the most celebrated works of art were removed to Paris, but in 1816 they were, with the exception of the colossal Melpomene, the statue of Augustus in the toga, the Velletri Minerva, and the Tiber, restored to the Vatican. Pius VII. added a long gallery of sculpture, which bears his name, Chiaramonti; a magnificent hall erected by the same Pontiff was opened in 1821, under the name of the Braccio Nuovo. It contains the beautiful Minerva Medica (No. 18), the Nile, already described, the standing Demosthenes (No. 321), the Faun of Praxiteles (No. 10), and the Little Ganymede of Phaidimos (No. 227).

THE CAPITOL MUSEUM,

The second collection of importance in Rome, was founded by Innocent X., continued by Clement XII., and considerably increased by Benedict XIV., and Clement XIII. Several of its figures were removed from the Vatican, and some of the choicest specimens from the Villa Ludovisi.

A few of the sculptures have been detained in Paris since 1816, among them the Nereid Sarcophagus (No. 140), and the Muses (No. 133).

THE FARNESE COLLECTION,

Founded by Paul III., became the property of the King of Naples upon the death of the Duke of Parma in 1786, and has been entirely transferred to Naples, where it is incorporated in the Museo Borbonico.

The principal Farnese treasures were the colossal Hercules, the so-called Flora, Dirce tied to the Bull, torso of Bacchus, and a statue of Antinous.

VILLA BORGHESE.

The collection of the Villa Borghese was sold by Prince Camillo Borghese in 1806 to his brother-in-law, Napoleon, and transported in 1808, entire, to Paris, where it is now incorporated with the other antiques of the Louvre. Since that time another rich collection has been formed at Rome to replace it.

VILLA ALBANI

Contains rich treasures, that formed the basis of Winckelmann's studies. A few of these passed to Munich, Paris, and Dresden. All the principal antiques will be found engraved in the "Monumenti inediti" of Winckelmann.

VILLA LUDOVISI

Still retains some very superior works of art found principally in the gardens of Sallust; they consist of the Mars, Orestes and Electra, or Penelope and Telemachus, and the group of Pætus and Arria, Pan teaching the young Olympus, together with two heads of Juno—one of them colossal—the other of an early style of art.

VILLA MEDICI

Formerly contained the celebrated statues now in the Florence gallery (see Florence).

PALAZZO SPADA

Possesses some very fine bas-reliefs, published also by Winckelmann and Dr. Emil Braun. The most important are Bellerophon and Pegasus, Paris and Helen, Pasiphae, Death of Archemorus, Meleager leaning on his spear. Also a very interesting sitting statue, regarded by Visconti as Aristotle. Part of the name is inscribed.

VILLA MONTALTO,

Founded by the Pope Sixtus V., contained many fine works. Among them the statues of Menander and Posidippus. The villa was afterwards called Negroni, and now Massimi. Most of the sculptures passed to the Museo Pio Clementino.

NAPLES.

MUSEO BORBONICO.

Naples is rich in antique works of every description. The most important source is the excavations carried on at Pompeii and Herculaneum, and discoveries continually made at Nola and Canosa. The Farnese collection already adverted to, and the sculptures forming the Museo Borgia, consisting of specimens found especially at Velletri, greatly contribute to the importance of the Studij as a resort for the learned.

FLORENCE.

GALERIA IMPERIALE IN THE UFFIZII

Contains several antiquities of great importance. The chief statues were in the Villa Medici at Rome until 1680 and 1775, when they were transported to Florence by the Grand Dukes, Cosmo III. and Peter Leopold. The principal statues are the Venus, the Apollino, Wrestlers, the series of Niobe, and the fine vase with the sacrifice of Iphigenia.

PISA.

THE CAMPO SANTO

Cloisters are adorned with a most splendid and interesting collection of sepulchral monuments, many of them are Sarcophagi of Roman times, with fables of the Pagan religion sculptured upon their sides, and from this source the illustrious sculptors Niccolo and Andrea Pisano, from A.D. 1200 to 1330, derived much of their inspiration. The front of a large Sarcophagus and a Bacchic Vase may be seen in this collection, Nos. 118 and 356.

FRANCE.

THE LOUVRE

Contains a rich collection of ancient sculpture founded by Francis I. He employed Primaticcio, a pupil of Giulio Romano, to visit Italy for the express purpose of purchasing antique statues. One hundred and eighty-four statues and numerous busts were acquired in this manner, and collected at Fontainebleau, which then became, in the words of Vasari, a second Rome. The celebrated Diana, No. 261, has been in France ever since this period. Henry IV. greatly increased the collection, and Richelieu and Montmorency procured many fine remains from Italy, some of which were deposited in the Château at Ecouen. Louis XIV. assembled the finest works of art at Versailles; and in 1796 the Louvre was destined to comprise the most celebrated antiques from all parts of Italy. The Borghese collection was transferred to Paris in 1808. but in 1816 nearly all the chef d'œuvres of Italy were restored. A few only remained from the Vatican, Capitol, and Villa Albani. The Count Choiseul and MM. Laborde and Texier have since contributed materially to increase the collection, various sculptures brought from Assos, Pergamos, and Magnesia, in the Meander, have been added to it. The most recent acquisition made is the series of Assyrian works of art procured by the zeal and enterprise of MM. Botta, Flandin, Mohl, and De Saulcy.

The chief private collections in France are those of the Duc de Blacas, Count Pourtalès, and Baron Beugnot.

ENGLAND.

Is rich in works of art. Private collections contain very fine specimens, chiefly through the energy of Gavin Hamilton, Brown, and Byres. Woburn Abbey, Marbury Hall, Ince Blundell, Petworth, Wilton House, Deepdene, and Lansdowne House, are among the richest with respect to these antiquities. The Arundel collection at Oxford, formed by the Earl of Arundel (1634), contained when entire 37 statues, 128 busts, and 250 inscribed marbles, exclusive of sarcophagi, altars, fragments, and gems.

THE BRITISH MUSEUM

Is the most recent of national collections of sculpture, and, in many respects, the most important of all.

Mr. Gavin Hamilton, a Scotch artist of considerable learning and ability, resident at Rome, in 1770, proposed to the Papal government to undertake excavations among the well-known ruins of former grandeur, and to share the results with them. An arrangement was thus entered upon. The antiquities were to be divided into four shares. The first to go to the Pope, the second to his ministers of state, the third to the possessor of the soil, and the fourth to the adventurer. By this means, the Popes Clement XIV. and Pius VI. acquired their rich treasures, which induced them to commence the celebrated Vatican Gallery, called the Museo Pio Clementino. A portion of these discoveries found their way to Great Britain, and were purchased by several private gentlemen, but principally by Mr. Townley.

Mr. Charles Townley, whose taste and accomplishments enabled him to appreciate the refinements and excellences of art, spared no pains or expense to procure the choicest specimens. He spent a considerable time in Rome, and devoted himself to watch the excavations, and finally deposited his rich collection at his residence in Park Street, Westminster. The most profitable excavations were made on the site of Hadrian's Villa at Tivoli (see page 14), at the ancient Gabii, Tor Columbaro, Albano, Velletri, and Ostia. Mr. Jenkins, the English banker at Rome, also materially assisted Gavin Hamilton.

On the death of Mr. Townley, in 1805, his collection of ancient marbles and terra-cottas was purchased by the nation for the sum of £20,000, and an additional edifice was built at the British Museum for their reception. It was opened to the public in 1808. Among the treasures thus acquired were the famous Dione (No. 3), a repetition of the Discobolus (No. 4), and also of Cupid bending his bow (No. 191).

The most important acquisition ever made of ancient sculpture took place in 1816, when England became possessed of the original marbles from the Parthenon, executed by the best artists of the finest period of Greek art. Nothing has ever since equalled them, and their shattered condition is on that account the more deeply to be lamented.

The Phigaleian, Lycian, Halicarnassian, and Assyrian marbles have been successively added, and their superior importance over all the bassi rilievi of Italy and other collections consists in the fact that the history of the buildings to which they belonged, and in which they had remained, is well known ; consequently, we are in possession of information respecting the period at which they were produced, and the artists who executed them. In Italy, on the contrary, detached fragments of Greek art are frequently discovered, but having been transported from some other country, all clue to their original connection is lost. Even in Hadrian's Villa everything is uncertain, from the fact that that Emperor is known to have delighted in copies, and to have had great numbers made when he was unable to transport the originals to his own halls.

THE ROYAL ACADEMY OF ARTS IN TRAFALGAR SQUARE.

Possesses a collection of the finest casts ever executed from the antique statues in Italy. Before the French conveyed the ancient marbles from Rome, a series of casts were taken with the utmost skill and precision from the originals, in order to supply their places on the pedestals of their prototypes. When the marbles were restored to Italy, the Sovereign Pontiff, in acknowledgment of the part undertaken by this country, presented the casts to the Prince Regent, by whom they were bestowed upon the Royal Academy.

MUNICH.

THE GLYPTOTHEK OR SCULPTURE GALLERY

At Munich consists principally of statues and reliefs purchased from the Villa Albani, and the Barberini, Roudanini and Braschi palaces. The Sleeping Faun, Ilioneus, Venus of Cnidos, and Alexander the Great, also the busts of Minerva, Medusa, and Laughing Faun, are among the principal treasures. The Ægina statues are second in importance only to the Parthenon marbles now in the British Museum, and were purchased by the ex-king in 1812.

BERLIN.

Contains few objects of especial celebrity. The bronze youth supplicating (No. 232), and the great Antinous (No. 314), are among the principal. The greater part came from Sans Souci and Potsdam, and were made up by Cavaceppi. The so-called family of Lycomedes, bequeathed by Cardinal Polignac, are in reality figures of the Muses converted by the restorer; but fortunately, at the suggestion of Levezow, the greater part have been made to resume their original appearance. The Polymnia (No. 50) is especially fine. No. 49 remains unaltered.

DRESDEN.

Contains two interesting statues of Minerva (Nos. 54 and 48), the base of a large candelabrum of elaborate workmanship, and many statues restored by Cavaceppi. A few figures from the first excavations at Herculaneum, and others from the Villa Albani. See p. 17 of description of Pompeian Court.

VIENNA.

Has few ancient works of importance in marble, with the exception of the torso of an Amazon, and the celebrated Fugger Sarcophagus (No. 58), found at Laconia. The collection of gems is the finest in existence. They have been ably illustrated by the Abbé Eckhel.

MADRID.

Possesses two ancient works of interest; one, the Young Faun carrying a goat, and the other a group of two figures, called Antinous and his Genius; both of which belonged to Christina, Queen of Sweden. The nine Muses, which were her property also, are for the most part modern.

LIST OF PRINCIPAL ILLUSTRATED WORKS ON SCULPTURE AND SERVICEABLE DESCRIPTIONS REFERRED TO IN THE CATALOGUES.

Admiranda Romanorum Antiquitatum, a P. S. Bartolo incisa, Notis Bellorii Illustrata, fol., Romæ, 1693.
Very spirited etchings of bas-reliefs and paintings in the usual bold style of Santi Bartoli, who was a pupil of Nicolas Poussin.

Ancient Marbles in the British Museum, 4to., London, 1812-45.
Excellently engraved plates from the truly artistic designs of Corbould.

Ancient Terra-cottas in the British Museum, 4to., London, 1810.

Annales du Musée, 17 vols., 8vo., Paris, 1801-9.

Annali dell' Instituto di Corrispondenza Archeologica di Roma, 8vo text, and large Atlas of Plates, 1829-54.

A valuable series of outline engravings, a few slightly shaded, of every new monument worthy of record, or admitting a fresh interpretation.

Antichita di Ercolano esposte, Pitture antiche d'Ercolano, 9 vols. Napoli, fol., 1757.

An admirable series of highly finished engravings, from both pictures and bronzes, worthy of note for their artistic freedom and faithfulness to the originals, a great contrast to the plates in the Museo Borbonico.

BARTOLI, P. S., Gli Antichi Sepolcri Romani, sm. fol., Rom., 1704.

BECKER, Augusteum des Monumens Antiques a Dresden, 3 vols., sq. fol., Leipsig, 1804-11.

Hard shaded plates, failing to express the style of the originals.

BELLORI, Veteres Arcus Augustorum, fol., Romæ, 1690.

BELLORIUS, Colonna Trajana, oblong fol., Roma, 1690.

BLEWITT's Handbook to Naples, Murray, 8vo., 1853.

BOUILLON, Musée des Antiques, 3 vols., fol., Paris.

By far the finest work that has ever appeared upon ancient sculpture. An excellent draughtsman has transferred his taste and skill upon the copper itself. Bouillon engraved all the plates of statues with his own hand, and has rendered with the most scrupulous exactness not only the forms but every perceptible variety of surface upon the sculpture. His points of view are, for the most part, admirably chosen. How far his talent suffered through other engravers may be seen in the plates of the Musée Français.

BRAUN, E., Antike Marmorworke, fol., Leipzig, 1843.

BRAUN, E., Zwölf Basreliefs Griechischer erfindung aus Palazzo Spada, Capitol und Villa Albani, fol., Rom., 1845.

Gracefully shaded large plates, which well exhibit the character of relief in these interesting sculptures.

BRAUN, E., Vorschule der Kunst Mythologie, Gotha, 1854.

BRÖNSTED, Voyages dans la Grèce, 2 vols., 4to., Paris, 1826-30.

Bronzi di Ercolano, Busti, Napoli, fol., 1767.

Bronzi di Ercolano, Statue, Napoli, fol., 1771.

BUNSEN, Beschreibung der Stadt Rom., 5 vols., 8vo., Stuttgart, 1830-42.

An invaluable work for information in every department, written in German. The antiquarian part chiefly by Gerhard and Platner.

CAUSEUS, Museum Romanum, vol. i., Divinités, fol., Romæ, 1746.

CAVACEPPI, Raccolta d'Antiche Statue, 3 vols., fol., Roma, 1768-72.

CLARAC, Musée de Sculpt. Paris, 8vo texte, 4to Atlas, 1826-51.

A very useful series of outlines of the Louvre sculptures and nearly all the statues extant, classed according to names of divinities and heroes. Foreign bas-reliefs are totally wanting.

CLARAC, Venus de Milo, et sur la Statue du Germanicus, 4to., Paris, 1821.

DELA CHAUSE (Causeus).

DENKMÄLER, der Alten Kunst, von Oesterley, oblong fol., Gottingen, 1832-54.

A most useful series of small outlines of the principal ancient monuments. The best for ready reference.

DESGODETZ, Edifices Antiques de Rome, folio, Paris, 1682.

Dilettanti Society's Specimens of Antient Sculpture, 2 vols., fol., London, 1809-35.

Profusely shaded drawings of sculpture in England only. Very important.

EASTLAKE, Literature of the Fine Arts, 8vo., London, 1848.
FABRETTI, de Columna Trajani, fol., Rom., 1683.
FAU, Anatomy for Artists, by Knox, Bailliere, Lond., 8vo., 1849.
The text, by Dr. R. Knox, contains many valuable criticisms upon antique statues, which, not being merely anatomical, may be read by every one.
FLAXMAN's Lectures, 8vo., Lond., 1838.
Galleria Giustiniana, 2 vols, fol., Roma, 1631.
GERHARD, Antike Bildwerke, fol., Munich, Stutgard and Tubingen, text, 4to., Munich, 1820.
Highly valuable plates of monuments in pure outline.
GERHARD, Archäologische Zeitung, 4to, Berlin, 1843-48.
A valuable record of new discoveries and opinions. The plates, for the most part in outline, are remarkably excellent.
GERHARD and PANOFKA, Neapels Antike Bildwerke, Stutgardt and Tubingen, 8vo., 1828.
GRUNER's Specimens of Ornamental Art, with Descriptions by Emil Braun, large folio, London, 1850.
Very important for the artistic accuracy and completeness both of form and colour with which everything is rendered.
GUATTANI, Monumenti Antichi inediti, 6 vols., 4to., Roma, 1784.
HIRT, Bilderbuch für Mythologie, Archäologie, und Kunst, 4to., Berlin, 1805.
HOPE, Costume of the Ancients, 2 vols., 8vo., London, 1841.
INGHIRAMI, F., Monumenti Etruschi o di Etruscho nome, 4to., Badia di Fiesole, 1820-4.
LAMBERTI, Sculture della Villa Borghese, 2 vols, 8vo., Roma, 1796.
*Le Musée Français, 4 vols., fol., Paris, 1803-9.
Large elaborate plates from excellent drawings, impaired by the engravers.
Le Musée Royal, par Henri Laurent, 2 vols., fol., Paris, 1816-8.
Shaded figures in a better style than the preceding.
LE PLAT, Receuil des Marbres Antiques qui se trouvent dans la Galerie du Roy de Pologne à Dresden, fol., 1 vol., 1733.
LEVEZOW, über den Antinous in den Kunst, 4to., Berlin, 1808.
Lucerne ed i Candelabri d'Ercolano, Napoli, fol., 1792.
LYON's Ægina Marbles, long fol., Liverpool.
Badly executed outlines.
MAFFEI, MuseumVeronese cui Taurinienses et Vindobonenses adjungitur, fol., Veronæ, 1749.
MAFFEI, Raccolta di Statue Antiche e Moderne, fol., Roma, 1704.
Serviceable for reference, but engraved without any regard to style.
Marmora Oxoniensia, sm. fol., Oxon., 1676.
MAZOIS, Les Ruines de Pompeii, fol., 2 vols., Paris, 1812.
MICALI, Monumenti inediti, fol. atlas, with 8vo. vol., Firenze, 1844.
MILLIN, Galerie Mythologique, 2 vols., 8vo., Paris, 1811.
A series of small outlines, chiefly copied from other publications, important as very generally referred to. A new edition, by Guigniaut, 1850, has appeared, but the figures of reference are altered, and I conceive it more acceptable to retain the old.

* The plates in the Musée Français, Musée Royal, and Wicar's Galerie de Florence are unfortunately not numbered, but the numbers of volumes have been carefully marked as they are bound in the British Museum Reading-room copy. The antique sculpture of the Musée Français is all collected in the last volume.

MILLIN, Monumens Antiques inédits, 2 vols., 4to, Paris, 1802.

MILLINGEN, Ancient Unedited Monuments, 4to, Lond., 1822.

Valuable especially for the style of illustration and sound system of explanation.

MONGEZ, Iconographie Romaine (a continuation of Visconti, whose work terminates with the period of the Republic).

MORI, Ricordi di Napoli, 8vo, 1843.

MÜLLER, C. O., Athenian Monuments, Hinterlassenen Papieren, von Adolf Scholl, Frankfurt, 1843.

MÜLLER, C. O., Archäologie der Kunst, edited by Welcker, 8vo, Breslau, 1848.

A highly important manual of antiquarian subjects and information. German text only.

MURRAY'S Handbook to Rome, 1853.

Highly valuable; both this and the Naples handbook contain a fund of information on all matters.

MURRAY'S Handbook to Greece, 8vo, 1854.

The Athenian portion written by Mr. F. C. Penrose.

Museo Borbonico, 15 vols., 4to., Napoli, 1824-53.

A series of small, slightly shaded outlines, from pictures, statues, and bronzes; text of little service, and the subjects chosen without discrimination; valuable only for reference as an authorised series. A surprising contrast to the magnificent work, "Antichità di Ercolano," mentioned above.

Museo Capitolino da Ferdo. Mori, 4to., Roma, 1806.

Museo Pio Clementino. (See Visconti.)

Museum Capitolinum, by Bottari and Foggini, 4 vols., fol., Romæ, 1741-82.

Carefully shaded engravings, and vigorously drawn, but the restorations not attended to.

Museum Florentinum, by Gori, Statues, 2 vols., fol., Florence, 1734.

Museum of Classical Antiquities, Edited by E. Falkener, Lond., 1852.

Containing valuable articles, by W. Lloyd, upon Polygnotos, Ch. Newton, upon collections of Ancient Art, E. Falkener, upon a Pompeian house, J. Hittorf, on the Polychromy of Greek Architecture, and G. Scharf, jun., upon Ancient Athenian Sculptures and the Polychromy of Sculpture.

PANOFKA, Terra-cotten des Museums zu Berlin, 4to, Berlin, 1841.

PENROSE, Principles of Athenian Architecture, published by the Society of Dilettanti, folio, London, 1851.

Picturæ Antiquæ, Criptarum Romanorum et Sepulcri Nasonum, fol., Romæ, 1750.

PISTOLESI, Il Vaticano, 8 vols., fol., Roma, 1829-38.

A very important series of lightly shaded outlines, of every variety of works of art; for the most part accurately drawn; the text of no antiquarian use whatever.

Pompeii, by A. T. Malkin, 2 vols., 8vo., 1831, published in the library of Entertaining Knowledge.

PONCE, Collection des Tableaux, &c. Trouvées à Rome dans les Thermes de Titus, fol., Paris, 1819.

Carefully engraved plates, the borders surrounding the larger composition, entirely made up.

PITTURE (see Antichita di Ercolano).

RAOUL ROCHETTE, Choix de Peintures de Pompeii, fol. (in progress), Paris, 1844-6.

A series of beautiful fac-similes of the paintings printed in full colours.

RAOUL ROCHETTE, Monumens inédits d'Antiquité, fol., Paris, 1833.

RAOUL ROCHETTE, Venus de Milo.

Revue Archéologique.

STUART'S Antiquities of Athens, edited by William Kinnaird, 4 vols., sm. fol., London, 1825.

Very valuable, containing much additional matter from recent discoveries, and with important information by Cockerell, Donaldson, and others.

THIERSCH, Über die Epochen der Bildenden Kunst, 8vo, München, 1829.

VAUX, Handbook to the Antiquities of the British Museum, 8vo., London, 1851.

Very useful as containing in one portable volume the most recent information with a series of bold and accurate woodcuts.

VISCONTI, Monumenti Gabini, 1797.

VISCONTI, Museo Pio Clementino, &c., 12 vols., 8vo., Milan, 1818.

Containing all the works of Visconti, except Monumenti Gabini, in simple outline. The large work from which this has been copied contains less information in text, and the plates, although very highly shaded, are of no service in expressing style or character.

VISCONTI, Notice des Statues du Musée Napoléon, 12mo., Paris, 1811.

WAAGEN, Treasures of Art in Great Britain, 3 vols., 8vo, 1854.

WELCKER, Alte Denkmäler, 3 vols., 8vo., Göttingen, 1849-51.

WELCKER, Zeitschrift der Alten Kunst, 8vo., Göttingen, 1817.

WICAR, Galerie de Florence, fol., Paris, 1789-1807.

Elaborately shaded engravings, in which style and character have been totally neglected. The text is neither serviceable to the artist nor the antiquary.

WINCKELMANN, Monumenti inediti, 2 vols., fol., Roma, 1767.

Notwithstanding the miserable style of the engravings, this work is especially valuable as a series often referred to, and the text worthy of regard, as produced by an antiquary who was the first to combat long-established prejudices and to place archæology as a science upon a firm basis.

WINCKELMANN, Sämliche Werke von Eiselin.

ZAHN, large folio, 2 vols., Berlin, 1828-9.

A very large work, with ornaments and pictures same size as the originals, beautifully coloured.

ZANETTI, Statues di S. Marco, 2 vols., fol., in Venezia, 1740.

ZANNONI, Reale Galleria di Firenze Illustrata, Seria IV., Statue e Bronzi, 3 vol. 8vo., Firenze, 1817.

A series of tame outlines not well selected.

ZOEGA, Bassi-rilievi Antichi di Roma, 2 vols., 4to., Roma, 1808.

Admirable outline engravings, by Piroli, and very sound criticism in text.

ZOEGA, Abhandlungen, von Welcker, 8vo., Göttingen, 1817.

ROMAN COURT CATALOGUE.

218. MODEL OF THE FORUM OF ROME.

Exhibiting the Capitoline Hill, the Ruins of the Temples of Saturn, Vespasian and Concord at its base; the arch of Septimius Severus, the column of Phocas, the Mamertine prisons, traces of the Basilica Julia, the Temple of Antoninus and Faustina, Church of S. Cosmo and Damian, the Temple of Peace, the Church of S.S. Francesco, Temple of Venus and Rome, the Coliseum, Arch of Constantine, Meta Sudans, Via Sacra, Arch of Titus, Palatine Hill, and three columns of the Comitium.

221. FAUN (SATYR), WITH RIGHT ARM RAISED.

Small life Statue. From DRESDEN.

Very like the one in the British Museum. A slender and noble form.

Restored by Rauch.

Engraved in Becker, Augusteum, No. 25; Le Plat, No. 16.

222. STATUE OF DRUSUS.

Greek Marble, life-size. From NAPLES. Found at Pompeii, with a statue of Livia, No. 273.

The flesh of the body somewhat hard in treatment. It greatly resembles the style of the Germanicus, No. 312.

Red colour still remains on the drapery of the original. Two statues of Tiberius and Germanicus, of Luna marble and heroic size, very similar to this and greatly resembling each other, were found at Gabii (see Mon. Gab. Nos. 5 and 7). Compare the arrangement of drapery in this portrait statue with that of the Youth, in No. 85.

Engraved in Mus. Bor. iii. 38; Comp. Visconti, Icon. Rom. 3, p. 24; H. B. p. 162, says Carrara marble instead of Greek.

Dimensions: Height, 6′· 3″·3·

223. YOUNG FAUN (SATYR), CARRYING A GOAT.

From MADRID. Discovered in Rome near the Church of Sta. Maria in Vallicella (S. Bartoli, Memorie, No. 68, 69, p. 315).

The trunk of tree at his side is very roughly carved, the *syrinx*, or shepherd's pipe, hanging on it, being merely, as sculptors would say, blocked in. His flourishing crown of fir is too like the hair; but I found, upon examining the beautiful cast in the Royal Academy (see page 25), that all that portion of crown seen in front remains as unfinished as the stem and syrinx just described, and that those effects which any thoughtful person would at once condemn, are solely attributable to modern plasterers and modellers.

Restorations: Both arms from shoulders, the pedum, and also left leg, from below knee to middle of the foot. The restorations were made by Ercole Ferrata.
Engraved in Maffei, tav. 122; Clarac, Musée, pl. 726 E, No. 1671 H.
Dimensions: Height, 4′· 6″· 0·

224. DRAPED VENUS (APHRODITÊ) AND CUPID (ERÔS).

Group, life-size, in Parian Marble. From the LOUVRE. Formerly in the Château de Richelieu.

The head and bust of the goddess are antique, but have been appropriated to this group. The peculiarity here is that Venus is draped, reminding one of the story told of Praxiteles having made two statues of Venus, one draped, the other naked. The name of Praxiteles is inscribed upon the original plinth, but it can only be regarded as an addition of a subsequent period to the execution of the figure. The group was originally a portrait of Roman personages.

Restorations: The nose, chin, and right fore-arm of Venus, and right arm and left hand of Cupid.
Engraved in Bouillon, vol. iii. pl. 6, No. 7; Cl. Cat. p. 85, No. 185; Clarac, Musée, pl. 341, No. 1291.
Dimensions: Height, 5′· 9″· 2·

225. YOUNG HERCULES (HÊRAKLÊS).

Small Statue of Parian Marble. From the LOUVRE.

Hercules a follower of Bacchus. Small standing figure crowned with vine, holding club downwards in his left hand. Remarkable for the freshness of its preservation. The work of a refined artist, firm and correct in execution, and full of animation; belonging to the best period of art.

Restorations: Both arms from above elbow, the right leg from above the knee-pan, and left leg.
Engraved in Bouillon, vol. iii. pl. 16, No. 4; Cl. Cat. p. 191, No. 485 Clarac, Musée, pl. 276, No. 1640.
Dimensions: Height, 4′· 5″· 3·

226. VENUS (APHRODITÊ) OF THE CAPITOL.

Statue, life-size, of Parian Marble. From the CAPITOL, in ROME. Found in a house in the Suburra. The only restorations are the nose and some of the fingers.

Flaxman (p. 25) says: "An example of more dignified and less insinuating beauty than the Venus de' Medici, certainly a copy from one of the three enumerated by Pliny among the works of Praxiteles." "The Venus is beautifully displayed; there is a purity about the general form more elevated to me than the one of Florence. The limbs are all thicker and less soft; the surface is pale and unpolished; even the extremities are quite unbroken, excepting two or three fingers that have been supplied in terra-cotta. The general style and turn of the head seems much more consistent with the rest of the figure than in the Medicean Venus. The hair only seems too bulky and heavy for the head. The turn of wrist and expression of the feet, as well as the uninjured neck, deserve especial attention" (MS. Journal, Rome, April 25, 1844).
A statue preferred by many to the Venus in the Medici collection, No. 198. It is hardly necessary to observe that the sentiment is perfectly different.

Notwithstanding the elegance of the forms, there is a coldness about the figure suitable rather to Diana than to Venus, and this opinion is also favoured by the peculiar arrangement of the hair, which closely resembles that of her brother Apollo in numerous statues. The goddess is just prepared to enter the bath, which is indicated by the drapery laid upon the vase, and under the same circumstances as when she was seen inadvertently by Actæon.

Engraved in Bouillon, vol. i. pl. 10; Mus. Capit. vol. iii. tav. 19; Bunsen, vol. iii. p. 252; Mori, vol. ii., Sala Grande, tav. 25. Musée Français.
Dimensions: Height, 6′· 0″· 2·

227. GANYMEDES.

Life-size, of Greek Marble. From the VATICAN. Found at Ostia, in 1805.

The statue when discovered was still in its original niche, ornamented with mosaic, where it served as a fountain; a channel for the passage of the water was made in the trunk, and communicated with the original pitcher to which it was attached, so that the water flowed through that aperture. Inscribed on the tree-stem ΦΑΙΔΙ ΜΟΣ.

Restorations: The fore-arms, hands, and vase.
Engraved in Visconti, vol. viii. tav. 11; Clarac, Musée, pl. 407, No. 703; Pistolesi, vol. iv. tav. 13; Bunsen, vol. ii. part 2, p. 103.
Dimensions: Height, 4′· 1″· 7·

228. VENUS GENITRIX.

Statue, life-size, of Parian Marble. From the LOUVRE. Previously in the gardens at Versailles.

This Venus is represented on imperial Roman coins with the inscription VENVS GENITRIX—see Sabina medals—because the Romans regarded her as the mother of their ancestors. The original of this statue has the ears bored for earrings. She holds the apple of Paris in her hand, and this also is seen on the medals. She is habited in thin and close-fitting tunic, which displays the contour of her limbs to great advantage; but the style of workmanship is hard, and wanting in sentiment, evidently copied from a superior original. Flaxman considered the original of this figure to have been the draped Venus of Cos, which the inhabitants purchased from Praxiteles (p. 91). A similar statue also from the Farnese Palace, now at Naples (Mus. Bor. vol. xiv. tav. 23). Another also at Holkham, restored with a vase in her left hand (Clarac, Musée, pl. 594, No. 1449 A).

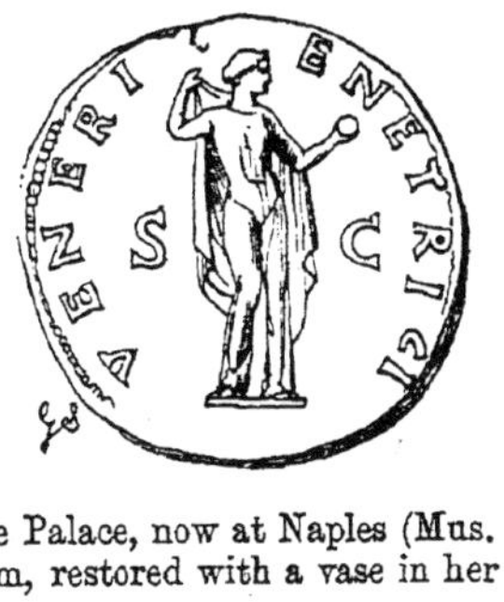

Engraved in Bouillon, vol. i. pl. 12; Gal. Nap. No. 57; Cl. Cat. p. 23, No. 46; Clarac, Musée, pl. 339, No. 1449; Compare a V. Genitrix at Florence, Gal. di Fir. vol. i. pl. 10, and a graceful V. Sabina in the Vatican, Mus. Pio Clem. vol. iii. tav. 8. Musée Français.
Dimensions: Height, 5′· 4″· 7·

229. GIRL, CALLED JULIA, DAUGHTER OF AUGUSTUS.

Statue, life-size, of Pentelic Marble. From the LOUVRE.

Portrait of a Roman girl of the early period of the Empire, as the hair is arranged according to the fashion then prevailing. Attitude graceful and draperies well adjusted and executed.

Engraved in Cl. Cat. No 481; Clarac, Musée, pl. 300, No. 2265. Musée Français. See Portrait Gallery, No. 95.
Dimensions: Height, 4′· 5″ 9·

230. PORTRAIT OF A MUSICIAN.

FEMALE PERFORMER ON THE LYRE.

Statue. From the LOUVRE.

The style of hair indicates this statue to be of the period of Trajan or Hadrian, the form of the lyre is elaborated, and not characteristic of purer times. She holds the *plectrum* in her right hand.

Restorations: Entire of left arm and most of lyre, right fore-arm and hand, several portions of drapery.
Engraved in Clarac, Musée, pl. 310, No. 2221; Clarac, Cat. p. 134, No. 314.
Dimensions: Height,

231. SMALL FEMALE FIGURE ATTIRED LIKE A VICTORY (NIKÈ).

Right hand raised, the left holds a wreath; the hair gathered in a large knot behind; a band descends across the body from the right shoulder. Very poor work; drapery common.

232. YOUTH INVOKING THE GODS—SUPPLICANT.

Bronze Statue, small life-size. From BERLIN.

Found in the Tiber, and presented by Clement XI. to Prince Eugene of Savoy. It was afterwards possessed by Prince Lichtenstein, who sold it to Frederick II. for ten thousand crowns. Some authorities say that it was found at Herculaneum previous to the discovery of the city; but this is unlikely, as everything in the latter place lay seventy feet below the modern surface of the soil, and was only to be approached by deep shafts for wells. Entirely naked, according to the custom of the gymnasts. He appears to be invoking success, perhaps before the games begin; there is much expression in the face. It is an interesting subject for comparison with the bronze boy of the Capitol, No. 247.

Restorations: Part of right arm and hand.
Engraved in Bouillon, vol. ii. pl. 19; Berlin Cat. No. 140, p. 13; Clarac, Musée, pl. 777, No. 1942; Mus. Nap. No. 237. Musée Français.
Dimensions: Height, 4′· 2″· 4·

233. MARINE VENUS AND CUPID.

From the LOUVRE.

Very like the Capitol Venus, No. 226, Cupid at her left stan ling on a Dolphin, and looking up pertly. He holds the dolphin's tail in his left hand.

Engraved in Villa Borghese, St. 5, No. 9; Cl. Cat. No. 174; Clarac, Musée, pl. 344, No. 1398.
Dimensions: Height, 6′· 0″· 7·

234. CAMILLUS.

A Bronze Statue. From the CAPITOL, at ROME.

Camillus, or boy attendant at sacrifices. Compare a similar bronze figure in Mus. Bor. vol. vi. tav. 8; and another with bronze extremities in Clarac, Musée, pl. 278, No. 1913; and Cl. Cat. No. 739. Eyeballs indicated by lines.

Engraved in Mus. Capit.; Mori; Maffei, tav. 24; Bunsen, vol. iii. p. 214.
Dimensions: Height, 4′· 7″· 6·

235. LARGE FEMALE FIGURE, CALLED MNÊMOSYNÊ.

From BERLIN.

Evidently the portrait of a Roman Lady. A broad band or kerchief passes over the upper part of her head, the drapery lies elegantly on the right shoulder, and is very well arranged; the execution of it is, notwithstanding, coarsely executed. The figure stands on a circular base, much corroded.

Engraved in Clarac, Musée, pl. 540, No. 973D.

236. VENUS (APHRODITÊ), WITH A FRONTLET ON HEAD, AND ARMLET.

From FLORENCE.

With the left hand she holds the drapery which envelopes the lower part of her figure, the right is raised to the hair, a bracelet on the right arm, and remains of red and gold are to be seen on the frontlet. A much admired statue, and, in the opinion of many, it ranks next to the Venus de' Medici.

Engraved in Gori, Mus. Flor. Statue, tav. 30; Florence Guide, p. 151; Meyer, Geschichte der Kunst, taf. 11, e.; Wicar, Galerie de Florence, vol. i.

237. VENUS (APHRODITÊ) VICTRIX.

Statue, heroic size, of Greek Marble of Mount Hymettus.
From the LOUVRE. Called VENUS OF ARLES.

This statue was found at Arles, in Provence, in 1651, and remained long at Versailles. The execution of the entire figure is admirable, the drapery excellent; but there is a deficiency in the general appearance when viewed as a whole. This Venus, so called from the place where she was discovered, is clothed only in the lower half of the figure; her head, rarely so well preserved, and of extraordinary beauty, is bound by a delicate band, which adds materially to the elegance. She is holding the apple of Paris in her right hand, and the handle of a mirror in the other. The town of Arles was a Roman colony, Municipium Arelatense, and therefore it would be natural to find the statue of the goddess from whom their founder was said to have sprung.

Engraved in Bouillon, pl. 13; Cl. Cat. p. 123, No. 282; Clarac, Musée, pl. 342, No. 1307; Mus. Nap. No. 138. Musée Français.
Dimensions: Height, 6′· 5″· 5·

238. VENUS (APHRODITÊ)—CALLIPYGOS (Καλλίπυγος).

Statue, life-size, of Greek Marble. From NAPLES. Formerly in the Farnese Collection at Rome. Found in the ruins of the Golden House of Nero.

Winckelmann places this statue in the second order of excellence. "The drapery is close, the folds are small, and at the lower part fall in particularly straight lines, like those in Rome, from the small temple of Minerva. The feet are beautifully pronounced; the knee-joint and adjacent parts slight and flat; the crease at the bend of the right arm long and sharp. The face approaches the L. da Vinci character, but the head and left arm are modern, restored by a Roman sculptor" (MS. Journal, Naples, April 20, 1844).

Restorations: The head, neck, and naked part of breast; right leg, right hand from wrist, left arm, and portion of drapery raised by that hand.

Engraved in Mus. Bor. No. 288; Clarac, pl. 611, No. 1352; Neapels, p. 119, No. 429; H. B. p. 171; Piranesi, tav. 7.

Dimensions: Height, 5′·2″·5.

239. URANIA.

Statue, life-size, of Carrara Marble. From the LOUVRE. Formerly in the Gallery at Versailles.

The body of this figure is alone antique; the head and arms were restored by Girardon, who crowned her head with stars, and destined a volume for her hand. It may have been originally a figure of Hope, raising her tunic, as in many other instances. This action is clearly indicated by the folds in the drapery, which are very well arranged.

Engraved in Bouillon, pl. 41; Cl. Cat. No. 321; Clarac, Musée, pl. 339, No. 1898. Musée Royal, vol. ii.

Dimensions: Height,

240. BACCHUS (DIONYSOS).

Statue, small life, of Marble. From BERLIN.

Standing naked, leaning the left elbow on a tall stem, encircled with vine-leaves and clusters. The right hand holds part of a thyrsus, and his head is crowned with ivy.

Engraved in Clarac, Musée, pl. 690 B, No. 1600 B.

Dimensions: Height, 4′· 10″· 0·

241. RICHELIEU BACCHUS (DIONYSOS).

Life-size Statue of compact Greek Marble. From the LOUVRE. It was brought from the Castle of Richelieu; hence it is known as the RICHELIEU BACCHUS.

The son of Semele wears a band called *credemnon*. One of the finest statues of Bacchus known.

Restorations: Right arm from above the elbow; also the left hand and fore-arm, and the lower part of the left foot. The right leg from knee to ankle.

Engraved in Bouillon, vol. i. pl. 31; Cl. Cat. p. 72, No. 154; Clarac, Musée, pl. 272, No. 1570. Musée Français.

Dimensions: Height, 6′· 2″· 4·

242. FAUN.

Leaning his right elbow on a wine-skin, or *askos*, which rests on a square pedestal.

The general attitude is strained and drunken, the caudal development is very small, and the ears, instead of being pointed, are round. The figure is said to come from Naples. ? modern.

243. VENUS (APHRODITÊ) AND CUPID (ERÔS).

Group in Parian Marble, of life-size. From the LOUVRE. It was previously in the Villa Borghese, and had belonged to Pope Julius III., and the Palazzo della Valle.

The goddess is arming herself with the sword and helmet of Mars, in which Cupid is assisting her. She has an armlet on her left arm. This group is in a wonderfully perfect condition, as the tip of the sword is the only restoration. But unfortunately a modern sculptor went over the entire surface with rasp and polisher, so as to destroy all the original delicacy. Clarac marks the right arm and the left leg from below the knee to the ankle as restored.

Engraved in Bouillon, vol. i. pl. 16; Villa Borghese, St. 5, No. 7; Cl. Cat. p. 83, No. 180; Clarac, Musée, pl. 343, No. 1399.
Dimensions: Height,

244. FEMALE READING A SCROLL, SEATED ON A SQUARE FOUR-LEGGED STOOL.

Statue, life-size. From BERLIN.

Called by some Calliope, and by others a Sibyl.

Engraved in Cavaceppi, vol. i. No. 45; Berlin Catalogue, No. 145; Clarac, Musée, pl. 534, No. 1121.
Dimensions: Height,

245. VENUS (APHRODITÊ).

Small Statue of Parian Marble. From the LOUVRE.

Of delicate and careful execution. Smaller than the Vatican Crouching Venus, as it is often called, No. 248. It has the right hand raised above the head.

Restorations: Tip of nose, the right hand, entire left arm and leg, the bottom extremity of the foot, and part of the thigh.
Engraved in Bouillon, vol. i. pl. 15; Cl. Cat. No. 698; Clarac, Musée, pl. 345, No. 1417. Musée Royal, vol. i.
Dimensions: Height, 2′· 3″· 2·

246. CUPID (ERÔS) AND PSYCHE, WITH WINGS.

From FLORENCE. Very inferior to No. 78. Found at Rome on the Cælian Hill during the pontificate of Clement X., according to S. Bartoli (Memorie, No. 53); or in 1666, according to other authorities.

Cupid has the bird wings, as usual upon all works of early art, and Psyche with the butterfly wings which are peculiar to her.

Restorations: Cupid—all the right leg, half the left, and the wings, but sufficient indications of them remained on the back. Psyche—all the surface below the knees, and more than half the wings.
Engraved in Galleria di Firenze, vol. i. tav. 43; Clarac, Musée, pl. 652, No. 1496; Wicar, Gal. de Florence, vol. i.; Gori, Mus. Flor. tav. 43, 44.

247. BOY EXTRACTING THORN.

A small Bronze Statue. From the CAPITOL.

Several holes in this statue, worn by time, were carefully mended in the 16th century. The rock support is entirely antique, and of one piece with the rest.

Visconti imagines it to be a young Greek victor in the races of the *stadium;* he states that young boys were allowed to race at the public games, and that youthful victors were honoured with statues. The perfect nudity of this figure is the best argument in favour of his opinion. The execution of the head and hair is an excellent instance of the refinement of ancient bronze workmanship; and altogether the figure may be regarded as one of the finest bronzes in existence.

Engraved in Mus. Cap; Maffei, tav. 23; Bouillon, vol. ii. pl. 19; Bunsen, vol. iii. p. 119; Clarac, Musée, pl. 714, No. 1702; Mus. Nap. No. 128, Musée Français.

Dimensions: Height, 2′· 4″· 2·

248. VENUS (Aphroditê).

Statue, less than life-size, of Pentelic Marble. From the Vatican.

It was found at the end of the last century at Salona, to the right of the road leading to Præneste. The vase and a portion of the plinth are antique. The following inscription is upon the plinth of the original.

ΒΟΥΠΑΛΟΣ ΕΠΟΙΕΙ.

It is, however, regarded as modern. At the moment of leaving the bath the goddess seems to be waiting for some one to throw a veil over her, or to be in the act of anointing herself.

Restorations: The end of right foot, the left hand, right fore-arm, the hair, and all the upper part of the head. The face has been unfortunately retouched by a modern hand. The bracelet remarked by Visconti is no longer to be seen. It was either removed during an improvement of the restoration at Paris, or since its return to Rome.

Engraved in Bouillon, vol. i. pl. 14; Mus. Pio Clem. vol. i. tav. 10; Pistolesi, vol. v. tav. 63; Clarac, Musée, pl. 629, No. 1414; Galleria Giustiniani, vol. i. No. 38; Bunsen, vol. ii. part 2, p. 203; Mus. Nap. No. 52. Musée Royal, vol. i.

Dimensions: Height, 2′· 7″· 6.

249. CERES.

A small standing figure, veiled.

250. ANCHIRHÖÊ.

Small Statue of Parian Marble. From the Collection of Baron Von Humboldt, at Tegel, Berlin.

Advancing the right foot and raising her dress with right hand. She holds a jar on the left shoulder. Perhaps Nausicaa. Pausanias describes a statue of Anchirhöê in accordance with the action of the present figure (Visconti, vol. iii. pp. 257-8). Compare Mus. Pio Clem. vol. iii. tav. 5A; and Ince Blundel Collection. The latter, from the Villa d'Este at Tivoli, bore the name ANCHYRRHÖÊ on the plinth. It is at present near Liverpool. See Waagen. Treasures of Great Britain, vol. iii. p. 257.

Engraved in Pausanias, lib. viii. ch. 31, p. 328 (Taylor); Bouillon, pl. 57; Cl. Cat. p. 35; Clarac, Musée, No. 73, p. 35. Anchirhöê was the daughter of Nilus, and wife of Belus, by whom she became the mother of Ægyptus and Danaus. See Danaid, No. 14.

251. NYMPH EXTRACTING A THORN.

Small Statue. From FLORENCE. Repetition of a Greek Marble statue found at Pompeii (Mus. Bor. vol. x. tav. 47).

Much restored; the head characteristically modern; probably one of a group which may be traced through the Vatican. The head turned over the left shoulder, but Visconti pronounces this modern. The same attitude and drapery will be found in a Vatican group of Satyr and Female (Mus. Pio Clem. vol. i. pl. 49). The antique head is seen in the Vatican example (Visconti, p. 332).

Engraved in Gall. di Firenze; Guide de Florence, p. 245; Gori, Statue, tav. 33; Clarac, Musée, pl. 609, No. 1351.

Dimensions: Height, 3′· 4″· 5·

252. BELVEDERE APOLLO.

Statue, heroic size, of Luni Marble. From the VATICAN.

It was found towards the close of the 15th century, among the ruins of Antium, on the sea-coast. Julius II., whilst a cardinal, purchased it, and retained it in his Palazzo Colonna, near the church of SS. Apostoli. It was afterwards transferred by this pontiff to the Belvedere of the Vatican; hence the name. This statue was excellently engraved by one of the Marc Antonio school, in the time of the great Raphael. The mutilations of the figure are here shown. M. Visconti produces a certificate attested by many professional judges, that the marble is not Luni or Carrara (p. 154); when the statue was in Paris, the most experienced mineralogists pronounced it to be unlike any Greek marble they were acquainted with (Bunsen, p. 158).

"*What a great idea it gives us of God, to think that He has created a human being capable of fashioning so divine a form!*" was the noble exclamation of Mrs. Siddons on first beholding the Apollo in the Louvre. No statue has commanded such universal admiration among artists, and notwithstanding the discussions raised with regard to its originality, all seem to recognise and acknowledge the excellence of the first conception. The fiery animation of the countenance, and the snaky treatment of the hair, point very strongly to the age of Lysippus (see page 41 of Introduction to Greek Court), and favour the supposition that it is an excellent copy executed in the Augustan age. German critics go so far as to perceive in the countenance evident traces of the features of Nero. The remarkable breadth of nose seems the only circumstance in their favour. Whenever Nero appears in the character of any of the deities, his peculiar fashion of wearing the hair is always the same. The original statue is admirably placed in the Vatican, in front of a niche of grey marble, and in a separate building from the rest of the sculptures.

The son of Latona has just discharged the fatal arrow against the serpent Python. The bow still remains in his firm left hand, and the god appears to be watching the effect of his vengeance. Indignation is expressed in his countenance, especially by the dilated nostril and the curled lip. The eye seems starting, and the hair, light and flowing, contributes powerfully to the expression. It is bound by a band or *strophium*, and gathered in a knot over the forehead, as seen in many statues of Apollo and Diana. A quiver hangs at his right shoulder, and his feet are adorned with rich sandals. His mantle or *chlamys* is fastened on his right shoulder. It falls chiefly on his left side, and is thrown over that arm, so as to display both his form and action with the utmost grace. A feeling of perpetual youth pervades the whole figure, and at the first glance, vigour, agility, and elegance, combined with a noble expression of indignation, impress the beholder. The trunk of the tree seems allusive to the ancient olive of Delos, and the serpent twining round it, is the emblem of health and medicine, of which he was the presiding genius. It may therefore have been the statue described by Pausanias, dedicated to the god in his medical capacity after the plague at Athens. It is most probably a copy from a bronze; the treatment and elaborate execution of the hair could not have been devised for a marble statue: the drapery hanging from the left arm confirms this opinion; it represents a single piece of stuff, forming loose folds which should correspond on both sides; but this is not the case: the sculptor did not venture, on account of the thinness of the marble, to follow the original in this respect: although in the bronze itself, nothing can have been easier. It is most likely a first-rate copy executed in the Augustan age. Flaxman remarks (p. 133): "The energetic Apollo Alexicacos, or the Driver away of Evil, commonly called Belvedere, is 'severe in youthful beauty;' he supplies Homer's description to the sight — his golden locks are agitated, his countenance is indignant— the quiver is hanging on his shoulder, and he steps forward in the discharge of his arrow." Again, in comparison he says (p. 139): "The boundaries of personal beauty are the Apollo and Hercules; a more slender form than the Apollo is *maigre*, and one more covered with flesh than the Hercules must be clumsy; as one in which the parts are more forcibly marked than in the Laocoon, would be a dissected figure."

Restorations: The entire right fore-arm and left hand were restored by Montorsolo, a pupil of Michel Angelo.

Engraved in front view by Agostino Veniziano, with the letters A · V, in the centre below, Bartsch, vol. xiv. No. 328; another view engraved by Marc Antonio, Bartsch, vol. xiv. p. 249, No. 330; Mus. Pio. Clem. vol. i. tav. 14; Bouillon, pl. 17; Pistolesi, vol. iv. tav. 106; Bunsen, vol. ii. part 2, p. 156; Maffei, tav. 2; Mus. Nap. No. 137.

Dimensions: Height, 7′· 2″· 0·

253. YOUNG FAUN (SATYR), PLAYING THE PIPE.

Small Statue of Parian Marble. From the LOUVRE. Previously in the Villa Borghese.

He rests with the *nebris*, or fawn-skin, upon a square plinth. A similar figure, somewhat smaller, belongs to the same collection; but it is of inferior art. Both, however, seem to have been copied from a much better original, perhaps suggested by the *Anapauomenos* of Protogenes.

Protogenes, the great Rhodian painter, represented a young faun leaning against a column, with a flute in his hand, whilst in the act of taking breath.

Restorations: The hands, part of flute, and head of the *nebris* are modern,

Engraved in Cl. Cat. p. 69, No. 146; Bouillon, vol. i. pl. 53; Clarac, Musée, pl. 296, No. 1671.

Dimensions: Height,

254. CUPID (ERÔS) AS THE REPOSING HERCULES (HÊRAKLÊS).

Small statue of Parian Marble. From the LOUVRE. Found at Gabii, whence it was transferred to the Borghese Collection at Rome.

Engraved in Bouillon, vol. iii. tav. 9, No. 2; Villa Borghese, Mon. Gal. No. 13; Cl. Cat. p. 123, No. 279; Clarac, Musée, pl. 282, No. 1478.

Dimensions: Height, 3′· 0″· 8·

255. HERCULES AND OMPHALE.

A small Group in Grechetto Marble. From NAPLES. Previously in the Farnese Collection.

Hercules clothed in a long tunic girded below the breast, and falling from the right shoulder, wearing a kind of long hood, and holding in his left hand a distaff, and spindle in the other. Omphale stands on his right, her head covered with the lion's skin, holding a club in her right hand. Well preserved and excellently wrought.

Restorations: The plinth and legs of both figures, right arm and club of Omphale, left arm and spindle of Hercules.

Engraved in Mus. Bor. vol. ix. tav. 27; Clarac, Musée, pl. 793, No. 1995; Neapels, p. 71; Gerhard, Ant. Bildw. pl. 29.

Dimensions: Height,

256. YOUNG FAUN (SATYR), PLAYING THE PIPE.

Statue. From the VATICAN.

One of the best among the numerous repetitions of this subject. It was found among the ruins of the villa of Lucullus in the Circæan Lake, where the waters had considerably damaged the surface of the statue. He is leaning with his left arm against the trunk of a tree. The *nebris*, fastened on the right shoulder, crosses over the left arm and falls down the tree-stem, which is more knotty than in the other repetition (No. 260). The statue is now in the Braccio Nuovo of the Vatican. The inscription on front of the pedestal is modern.

Engraved in Pistolesi, vol. iv. tav. 24; Bunsen, vol. ii. part 2, p. 95; H. B. p. 409.

Dimensions: Height,

257. FAUN (SATYR) ASKOPHOROS.

Small Statue. From the VILLA ALBANI, at ROME.

With pointed ears, carrying a wineskin or *askos* on his left shoulder, which he tilts forward to pour out the liquor. A great part of the wineskin and legs from above halfway up the thighs are entirely restored.

Praxiteles is said to have made a group of Pan, carrying a leather bottle, surrounded by the Nymphs. (Sillig. s. v. Praxit, No. 7, p. 110.)

Engraved in Clarac, Musée, pl. 704 c, No. 1730.

Dimensions: Height, to top of head, 3′· 9″· 3·; to top of skin, 3′· 10″· 3·

258. APOLLO SAUROCTONOS.

Size small half-life; no Lizard. From the LOUVRE.

The head large in proportion to the rest of the figure. Not so large as the other repetitions (see No. 373).

Engraved in Clarac, Musée, pl. 268, No. 905; Cl. Cat. No. 19; Bunsen, vol. iii. part 2, p. 518.

259. FAUN (SATYR) AND YOUNG PAN (PANISCUS).

Small Group in Parian Marble. From the LOUVRE. Formerly in the Borghese Collection, at Rome.

Of very inferior workmanship, but full of character and skilful composition.

No doubt from a superior original, as other repetitions are known to exist. Both these figures have tails.

Restorations: The right shoulder and arm and part of the left arm of the Faun are modern.

Engraved in Bouillon, vol. iii. pl. 13; Villa Borghese, St. 4, No. 12; Cl. Cat. No. 290; Clarac, Musée, pl. 297, No. 1741.

Dimensions: Height, 2′· 1″· 6·

260. YOUNG FAUN (SATYR), PLAYING THE PIPE.

A small Statue of Parian Marble. From the LOUVRE. Formerly in the Borghese Collection at Rome.

It is very similar in attitude and accessories to No. 256, from the Vatican, with the exception that the trunk of the tree is singular, and the plinth on which he stands is round. The general character of the figure is more erect than the other two.

Restorations: The flute and fingers of both hands.

Engraved in Bouillon, vol. iii. pl. 12, No. 2; Maffei, tav. 80; Clarac, Musée, pl. 296, No. 1670.

Dimensions: Height,

261. DIANA (ARTEMIS).

Heroic Statue of Parian Marble. From the LOUVRE. Previously at Versailles. With her left hand she holds a stag by the horns; hence the common French name for the group, LA DIANE À LA BICHE. It is also called DE VERSAILLES.

The exact time at which this statue came into France is not known, nor is there any record of the place where it was first discovered. Most probably it was brought from Italy by Primaticcio, in the reign of Francis I. The statue represents Diana, in the dress of a huntress, without sleeves, girded up above the knees, with a scarf or *chlamys* rolled like a sash round her waist, and passed belt-like over her left shoulder, holding the bow down in her left hand, whilst with the right she is about to draw an arrow from the quiver at her back. The legs are bare, but the feet are adorned with elegant sandals. A small frontlet or diadem surmounts her hair, which is gathered into a knot behind. The hind at her left side is very ingeniously contrived to serve as a support to the arm, for the horns of the animal are almost entangled in the bow which the goddess holds in her hand. The same clever connection of parts may be observed in the contact of the right arm with the quiver. From the circumstance of the hind being furnished with horns, we perceive in this animal no mere symbol of the chace, but the stag of Ceryneia in Arcadia, which, although a female, had horns of gold and brazen feet. It had been dedicated to Diana by the nymph Taygete, and its capture formed the third labour of Hercules. When on the point of bearing it off, Diana descended and took away the prize, and only restored it to the hero after earnest prayers and supplications. There is a striking similarity between this statue and the celebrated Apollo of the Belvedere (No. 252) in size, execution, and general sentiment. Both seem excited by anger, and have recourse to their peculiar weapons to avenge (No. 2 of Mus. Nap.), and may not improbably have been connected with other figures relating to the punishment of Niobe, as seen in a bas-relief of the Villa Albani (Zoega) and a sarcophagus in the Vatican (Mus. Pio Clem. vol. iv. tav. 17).

Restorations: The left arm is entirely modern; the right arm was much broken, but is original. The stag was much injured, and has been very well restored. The tip of nose and extremities were quite destroyed.

Engraved in Mus. Bouillon, vol. i. pl. 20; Landon, Annales du Musée, vol. viii. pl. 72; Cl. Cat. p. 81. No. 178; Clarac, Musée, pl. 284, No. 1202. Musée Français.

Dimensions: Height, 6′· 7″· 0·

262. BOY AND GOOSE.

From the LOUVRE.

Engraved in Clarac, Musée, pl. 293, No. 2226; Clar. Cat. No. 694; a similar group at Munich, Clarac, Musée, pl. 875, No. 2232; Glyptothek, No. 123.

263. BOY AND BIRD.

Sitting on the ground, he holds the duckling beneath his left hand, and is pressing it to the ground. The bird is struggling. Numerous repetitions of this group are known; a second one, apparently similar in every respect, is in the Florence gallery also.

Engraved in Mus. Pio Clem. 3, tav. 36; Gall. di Fir. vol. ii. pl. 70 and 71; Pistolesi, vol. vi. tav. 43; Clarac, Musée, pl. 877, No. 2229.

Dimensions: Height, 1′· 9″·

264. BOY WITH MASK.

From the Museum of the CAPITOL, at ROME.

A boy, sitting upon a pedestal covered with a goat-skin, is in the act of putting on a Silenus mask. Full of nature, and a good work of art.

Restorations: The right hand and both legs.

Engraved in Mus. Capit. vol. iii. tav. 40; Mori. vol. ii. Stanza dell' Ercole, tav. 6; Clarac, Musée, pl. 540, No. 1134; Bunsen, vol. iii. p. 246.

265. URANIA.

Small sitting Statue. From the VATICAN. Found in 1774, at la Pianella di Cassio, the site of a villa of Cassius, near Tivoli.

When discovered, this beautiful statue had neither head nor arms. Visconti says if this statue be smaller than the other Muses, it surpasses them in beauty and delicacy of execution. Found at Cassiano (text, p. 217). (See Visconti's notes on the drapery also, at p. 222.) The Muse of Astronomy is seated on one of the rocks of Mount Parnassus; the two feathers over her forehead are some of those which the Muses plucked from the Sirens when they presumed to compete with them. She is holding a globe in one hand, and a radius or wand in the other, both emblems of the science over which she presides. Her tunic has no sleeves, and one side falls gracefully lower on her left arm; it is fastened with a *fibula* on the right shoulder. The lower part of the drapery is doubled, and the transparency of the folds, and their delicate arrangement and execution, merit especial attention.

Engraved in Mus. Pio Clem. vol. i. tav. 25; Bouillon, pl. 46; Pistolesi, vol. v. tav. 42; Mus. Nap. No. 90.

Dimensions: Height, 2′· 10″· 3·

266. PENELOPE, RESTORED AS A CERES.

Small life Statue. From BERLIN.

Sitting on a four-legged stool, with the right hand planted on the seat. It is very similar to a figure in the Pompeian painting (Mus. Bor. 9, 51) and to the Penelope representations in terra-cotta, both in the British Museum and Millin's Mon. Inéd.

Restorations: Parts of face, the hand with flowers, and legs of stool.

Engraved in Clarac, Musée, pl. 429, No. 772; British Museum, Terra Cottas, No. 12, pl. 8; Millin's Mon. Ined. vol. ii. pl. 41, p. 317.

Dimensions: Height,

267. GANYMEDES, WITH BIRD AND EAGLE.

A small Statue. From FLORENCE. Restored by Benvenuto Cellini.

This figure displays in the strongest light the difference between genuine antique art and that of the 15th century. The curly hair and countenance of Ganymedes have all the peculiarities belonging to Da Vinci and Correggio: the expression is mischievous, and the clever Florentine, in placing a little fluttering bird in the hand of the boy, for purposes of torment, thought little of the signification of the fable he professed to illustrate. The money-bags also on the ground are a strange and unclassical accessory, and but for the words of Cellini himself, we might doubt his ever having meant the figure for Ganymedes at all. It is almost superfluous to add that the figure becoming a Ganymedes was an arbitrary matter with the sculptor. He might with greater propriety have placed a pitcher in the upraised hand. Ganymedes was often represented in ancient art giving drink to the bird of Jove.

Restorations: The only original part is the mere trunk of the figure (Mus. Pio Clem. vol. ii. p. 252 of text).

The following extract is taken from Cellini's own account of himself, as the best explanation of the artist's intention:—" 'Take this little chest, which was sent me as a present by Signor Stefano, and let us see what it contains.' I instantly opened it, and answered the duke, 'This, my lord, is the figure of a little boy in Greek marble, and is indeed a very extraordinary piece. I don't remember ever having seen amongst the antiques so beautiful a performance, or one of so exquisite a taste; I therefore offer your excellency to restore its head, arms, and feet, and make an eagle for it, that it may be called a Ganymede; and though it is by no means proper for me to patch up old statues, as that is generally done by a sort of bunglers in the business, who acquit themselves very indifferently, the excellence of this great master is such that it powerfully excites me to do him this piece of service.' "

Engraved in Gori, Mus. Flor. Statue, tav. 5; Gall. di Firenze, vol. ii. pl. 103; Galerie de Florence, Wicar, vol. i.

Dimensions: Height, 3'· 0"· 3·

268. GIRL, PLAYING AT OSSELETS, OR ASTRAGALS.

Statue, life-size, of Grechetto Marble. From BERLIN. Found at Rome, on the Cælian Hill, in 1730. Formerly in the Polignac Collection.

The game of knuckle-bones was a very favourite one with the ancients, and chiefly among women and children: it consisted in throwing the bones up in the air, and catching them on the back of the hand. Polygnotus painted the two daughters of Pandarus playing at this game, and a picture on marble was found at Herculaneum with females engaged in the same manner. A group in sculpture of two boys playing is in the British Museum, and Polycletus executed a fine bronze of two boys at this game, called *Astragalizontes.* Pliny saw them in the palace of Titus. The knuckle-bone was called *astragalos* by the Greeks, and *talus* by the Romans. They were the bones of sheep and goats. These have been found in the tombs. They were often made artificially of ivory, bronze, glass, and agate.

Restorations: The right hand, neck, left shoulder, and the two osselets on the ground.

Engraved in Bouillon, vol. ii. pl. 30; Berlin. Cat. No. 74, p. 7; Clarac, Musée, pl. 578, No. 1249. Musée Français.

Dimensions: Height,

269. BOY AND GOOSE.

Statue of Pentelic Marble. From the CAPITOL. Found at Roma Vecchia in 1789, on the Via Appia, at a place called Pagus Lemonius. Compare 262.

A modern inscription on the pedestal. "Munificentia, S.S.D.N., Benedict Pii, &c." The hair of boy is more worn than in No. 262. Eyeballs are indicated. The goose's beak is turned towards boy's face. This has a much more genuine surface than the other.

Pliny mentions Boëthus having made a boy strangling a goose: "Boëthi puer eximiè anserem strangulans."—Hist. Nat. lib. 34, 8, 19, 23. Four repetitions of this group, exactly alike, were found in the same locality.

Engraved in Bouillon, vol. ii. pl. 30; compare Pistolesi, vol. vi. tav. 36; Mus. Capit. vol. iii. tav. 64; Mori, vol. ii. Stanza dell' Ercole, tav. 7; Clarac, Musée, pl. 874, C. No. 2227 A; Munich Glyptothek, No. 123, formerly in Palazzo Braschi; Munich, one in Clarac, Musée, pl. 875, No. 2232; Bunsen, vol. iii. p. 247; Mus. Nap. No. 219. Musée Français.

Dimensions: Height, 2′· 9″· 9·

270. EUMACHIA.

A Statue, life-size, in white Marble. From POMPEII.

Found, 1820, in the Chalcidicum at Pompeii, where this statue had been erected by the dyers. She was a public priestess, and patroness of the Fullonica at Pompeii. The original pedestal is inscribed on the front—

EVMACHIAE·L·F
SACERD·PVBL.
FVLLONES.

Engraved in Gell's Pompeiana, 2nd Series, vol. i. page 21; H.B. page 159.

Dimensions: Height, 6′· 1″· 2·

271. PUDICITIA.

Statue, life-size, of Parian Marble. From the LOUVRE. Formerly in the Gallery at Versailles.

The figure is wrapped in a thick kind of mantle called *gausapa.* It came into fashion in the age of Augustus, and was worn indifferently by both sexes. Sometimes it was made of the finest wool, and occasionally of linen. This garment in the statue before us is remarkable for the length of fringe upon the border. The figure is not free from affectation, and seems to have suffered under the restorations effected by Girardon. The soles of the sandals are high enough for the *cothurnus*, but the restorer has forgotten to add the usual ligatures upon the foot. Compare Mus. Capit. vol. iii, tav. 44; Bunsen, vol. iii. part 1, p. 235.

Engraved in Clarac, Musée, pl. 331, No. 1885; Clarac, Cat., p. 60, No. 124.
Dimensions: Height,

272. PORTRAIT STATUE OF A ROMAN LADY.

Bronze, life-size. From the GLYPTOTHEK. A remarkably fine work.

The pallium is adjusted with great skill, to display the forms beneath it. There is much dignity in the countenance, increased by the elegant arrangement of the hair, and proportion of the frontlet. The surface of the bronze has suffered much from efflorescence, while it remained underground.

Dimensions: Height,

273. LIVIA DRUSILLA.

The wife of the Emperor Augustus. A Statue, life-size, of Grechetto Marble. Found at Pompeii, in the house of the Augustals or Pantheon, 1821.

This statue, and another of Drusus her son, No. 222, were found prostrate on the ground, near two niches that formerly contained them. The empress is represented as in the art of sacrificing; her head is encircled by a rich crown, probably of gold, and veiled with part of the pallium, or palla, drawn over it. The *stola* was a long dress reaching to the feet and worn over the tunic; it had a kind of flounce at the lower part. Sleeves were sometimes attached to it, and a girdle was generally fastened round the waist. A *fibula* or clasp was employed to fasten it at the shoulders. The *stola* for women corresponded to the *toga* for men. In her left hand she holds a small vessel, *acerra*, containing incense. The right fore-arm is wanting. A similar incense box in Clarac. Musée, pl. 886, No. 2269. Compare an ancient painting in the Villa Albani at Rome of Livia and Octavia sacrificing (Winckelmann, Mon. Ined. No. 177.)

Engraved in Mus. Bor. vol. iii. tav. 37; Clarac, Musée, pl. 918, No. 2342A; H. B. p. 350.

274. VASE.

From NAPLES. Museo Borbonico, with diagonal fluting, and figures on that.

275. CANDELABRUM.

Of Pentelic Marble. From the LOUVRE. Originally in the Vatican.

The triangular base is ornamented with ox-skulls on the sides, and hoofs at the angles. Salle de la Paix. Remarkable for the elegance and beauty of the leaves around it.

Engraved in Bouillon, vol. iii. Candelabres, pl. 3, No. 2; Cl. Cat. p. 45, No. 85; Clarac, Musée, pl. 257, No. 643; Mus. Nap. No. 185.

AT THE EXTREME NORTH END OF NAVE.

ÆGINA MARBLES.

From MUNICH. Statues not quite life-size, of Parian Marble. They occupied the two pediments of the Temple of Minerva, at Ægina.

These sculptures were discovered by Baron Haller, Messrs. Cockerell, Forster, Linkh, and Von Stackelberg, in 1811. They had been thrown down by an earthquake, and were shattered into numerous pieces. The entire collection was purchased by the King of Bavaria in 1812, and restored at Rome by the celebrated sculptor, Thorwaldsen. They were arranged according to the theory of Mr. Cockerell, and are now among the most interesting monuments of the Glyptothek. The remains from the western end are the most numerous, but those of the eastern are on a larger scale, and much better executed. The subject of the western pediment is the Contest of the Greeks and the Trojans, around the body of Patroclus. Minerva herself appears in the centre, completely armed, filling the entire height of the pediment. The differences of costume between the Greeks and Asiatics are characteristically observed. Paris is recognized by his tall cap and close-fitting dress. This was originally painted to give the appearance of scales such as may be seen in the armour of some of the Assyrian soldiers upon the bas-reliefs. The hair was partly composed of wire, and the holes remain in the marble which indicate where gilded bronze was originally attached. Traces of colour are to be found upon the hair, eyes, lips, clothes, weapons, and wounds. The temple itself, which was built of yellowish sandstone, was also painted in bright colours. The cella was painted red, the tympanum blue, with yellow and green foliage on the architrave. The small female figures stood on either side of the Acroteria in the centre. The angles were ornamented with griffins and lions' heads.

Engraved in Clarac, Musée, pl. 815, No. 2051; *ib.* pl. 821, No. 2063; and Lyons' Ægina Marbles.

STATUES IN THE NAVE ARRANGED IN FRONT OF THE GREEK AND ROMAN COURTS.

276. TORLONIA HERCULES.

Colossal Statue of Greek Marble.

Engraved in Clarac, Musée, pl. 790, No. 1970.

277. DOG, FROM FLORENCE.

A similar one in the Vatican. Molossus.

Engraved in Pistolesi, vol. iv. tav. 100.
Dimensions: Height, 3′· 8″· 5.

278. COLOSSAL CUPID, AS HERCULES.

Colossal Statue of Green Basalt. From the CAPITOL, at ROME. Found, according to Flaminio Vacca, upon the Aventine Hill, in the Vigna of Monsignor de' Massimi, near Monte Testaccio.

The head is covered with a lion's skin, tied round the neck. At Rome, the original figure stands upon the square altar with reliefs of the birth of Jupiter (See No. 205).

Restorations: The right fore-arm and left hand holding the apples of the Hesperides.

Engraved in Mus. Capit. vol. iii. tav. 26; Mori; Maffei, tav. 19; Bunsen, vol. iii. p. 229: Clarac, Musée, pl. 781, No. 1956.

Dimensions: Height, 6′· 8″· 1·

279. BACCHUS (Dionysos).

Statue, life-size, of Parian Marble. From the Louvre.

The antique portions of this statue were chiefly destroyed, and have been miserably restored. It must have originally been a very fine figure.

Engraved in Bouillon, vol. iii. pl. 7, fig. 1; Cl. Cat. No. 203; Clarac, Musée, pl. 272, No. 1571.

280. ANTINOUS.

Statue of Carrara Marble. From the Capitol, at Rome. Found in Hadrian's Villa. Presented by Cardinal Alexander Albani to Clement XII.

The favourite of the Emperor Hadrian was drowned in the Nile, A.D. 122. The young and handsome Bithynian is represented in the period of adolescence. The attitude and arrangement of the hair is evidently meant to represent Mercury. The right hand originally held a caduceus. This accords with other known statues of the deity Antinous is here made to personify. Notwithstanding his extreme youth, there is a melancholy expression in the downcast face. In other statues, No. 288 for instance, and on coins, the hair is treated in a very different manner.

Restorations: The right leg has not been properly readjusted; all below the right knee is modern; the left foot, the left fore-arm, and two fingers of the right hand have been restored.

Engraved in Mus. Cap. vol. iii. tav. 56; Bouillon, vol. ii. pl. 49; Mori, vol. ii. Stanza dell' Ercole, tav. 4; Visconti, Icon. Grecque; Bunsen, vol. iii. p. 251. See Portrait Gallery, No. 79.

Dimensions: Height, 6′· 6″· 7·

281. AGRIPPINA THE ELDER.

Life-size Statue, of Grechetto Marble. From Naples. Formerly in the Farnese Palace, at Rome.

The costume is very simple, consisting of a tunic, with short buttoned sleeve, and a mantle thrown over it. The hair, as seen on her coins, is very artistically arranged, and gathered in a knot behind. The drapery is excellent. The expression of face, and indication of age in the features, scarcely accord with the slender grace and ease of the rest of the figure. The feet, one crossed over the other, rest negligently upon a footstool. A workbasket or *calathus* beneath the chair, which is cleverly arranged to serve at the same time as a support to the marble figure.

Restorations: Only the hands and the footstool.

Engraved in Mus. Bor. iii. 22; H. B. 162; Neapels, 43, No. 124; Clarac, Musée, pl. 929, No. 2363. Comp. sitting Agrippina, of Villa Albani and the Capitol. See Portrait Gallery, No. 96.

Dimensions: Height, 4′· 0″· 2·; Length, 4′· 6″· 8·

282. **ADONIS.**

Statue, life-size, of Grechetto Marble. From the VATICAN.

Found on the Via Labicana in 1780, among some ruins called Centocelle. Pius VI. placed it in his museum. It was much broken, but well restored by Albacini. Both arms were wanting from the shoulders, the entire right leg, the left foot, and tip of the nose. The head had been separated. Visconti says that the inclination of the head is a sign of apotheosis (p. 229). Probably this statue was originally an Apollo, or an Erôs. It has wonderful grace about the shoulders.

Engraved in Mus. Pio. Clem., vol. ii. tav. 32; Bouillon, vol. ii. pl. 12; Pistolesi, vol. v. tav. 74; Clarac, Musée, pl. 633, No. 1424 A; Bunsen, vol. ii. part 2., p. 204; Mus. Nap., No. 118. Musée Français.
Dimensions: Height, 5′· 8″· 1·

283. **BACCHUS.**

Statue life-size. From BERLIN.

The god is crowned with ivy, and holds a patera in his right hand to a panther on the ground at his feet. The figure is naked, except a *nebris* or fawn-skin cast over the left arm, which is raised as the hand grasps the rod of a thyrsus. The antique portion is remarkably fine.

Restorations: Head, arms, legs, and tiger.
Dimensions: Height, 5′· 2″· 8·

284. **FAUN (SATYR) OF THE CAPITOL, WITH GOAT, PEDUM, AND CISTA.**

Rosso Antico. From the CAPITOL, at ROME. Discovered in Hadrian's Villa.

Restorations: The right arm and grapes, the left hand with pedum, thigh, and leg; the foot is ancient. The head of goat, portion of its neck, and tree-stem with syrinx are also modern.
Engraved in Mus. Capit. vol. iii. tav. 34; Bunsen, vol. iii. p. 241; Clarac, Musée, pl. 706, No. 1685; compare a better preserved statue in the Vatican Mus. Pio Clem. vol. i. tav. 46; Mus. Cap. vol. iii. tav. 33; Cavaceppii vol. i. No. 28.
Dimensions: Height, 5′· 2″· 7·

285. **MERCURY (HERMÊS).**

Reposing, with his right arm upon the trunk of a tree, over which a skin is hung. The right foot is crossed in front of the other. From FLORENCE.

Restorations: The greater part of the petasus, the right arm from below the elbow, the left also, a portion of the left thigh in front, above the knee, and part of the knee itself.
Engraved in Gori, Mus. Flor. Statue, tom iii. tav. 38; Gall. di Firenze, vol. iii. tav. 130: Maffei, tav. 57; Clarac, Musée, pl. 660, No. 1518.
Dimensions: Height, 4′· 10″· 8·

286. **TRAJAN, SITTING, HOLDING A GLOBE.**

Life-size, of Pentelic Marble. From ROME. Formerly in the Villa Mattei.

The head, although antique, does not belong to the statue; the hand and globe a modern addition, and one of the feet also has been restored. The figure seems to have been originally that of a philosopher sitting upon a simple chair (certainly not *curule*), covered with a cushion.

Engraved in Mus. Pio Clem. vol. iii. tav. 7; Bouillon, vol. iii. pl. 19; Cl. Cat. No. 95; Clarac, Musée, pl. 337, No. 2415. See Portrait Gallery, No. 45.
Dimensions: Height, 4′· 5″· 4·

287. MERCURY OF THE VATICAN.

Same as No. 316, with the exception that the drapery has been clumsily restored.

288. ANTINOUS.

Statue, life-size, in Grechetto Marble. From NAPLES. Formerly in the Farnese Collection at Rome.

The celebrated Bithynian Ganymede is here represented in the attitude of Mercury. So also the famous Capitoline statue, No. 280. The eyeballs are marked. Well worthy of the fame this statue has acquired.

Restorations: The arms and legs. See Portrait Gallery, No. 79.
Engraved in Mus. Bor. vol. vi. tav. 58; Neapels, p. 107, No. 367.
Dimensions: Height,

289. MELEAGER OF BERLIN, WITH DOG AND SPEAR.

Statue, heroic size, of Greek Marble. From BERLIN. Found at Sta. Marinella, near Civita Vecchia. Formerly in the Collection of the Duchess of Sermoneta.

Engraved in Clarac, Musée, pl. 811A, No. 2020 B; Berlin Catalogue, No. 33.

290. MENANDER.

Sitting Statue, life-size, of Pentelic Marble. From the VATICAN.

Found, together with Posidippus (No. 291), on the Viminal Hill, at Rome, in a circular hall, supposed to have belonged to the baths of Olympias. Sixtus V., in whose reign they were discovered, placed them in his Villa Negroni or Montalto. They were afterwards purchased for the Vatican by Pius VI. A large iron nail was fixed at the top of the head of both figures, for the attachment of a circular plate or *meniscus*, which was used to protect statues exposed in the open air, Bunsen, 171; but the introduction of the iron nail seems to have touched the cleavage of the stone and entirely separated the mask from the rest of the head. It had evidently been reattached with great care. See essay, by G. Scharf, jun., in the Trans. of Royal Soc. Lit. 1853. Menander is seated on a chair, called *hemicycle*, from the semicircular shape of the back; his portrait is identified by means of an inscribed bas-relief, by Visconti. The face is beardless, but very characteristic. He is resting his left arm upon the back of the chair. His tunic is partly covered up by the large square mantle or *pallium*; the general adjustment of his garments accords with the tradition of his carefulness in dress.

Restorations: Left hand and ring.
Engraved in Mus. Pio Clem. vol. iii. tav. 15; Bouillon, vol. ii. pl. 25;

Pistolesi, vol. v. tav. 45 ; Visconti, Icon. Grecque, vol. i. tav. 6; Bunsen, ii. part 2, p. 169 ; Clarac, Musée, pl. 841, No. 2118 ; Mus. Nap. No. 76 ; Musée Français. See Portrait Gallery, No. 32.

Dimensions : Height, 4′· 7″· 6·

291. POSIDIPPUS.

Sitting Statue, life-size, of Pentelic Marble. From the VATICAN.

Found with the Menander (No. 290), on the Viminal Hill, at Rome, in the reign of Sixtus V., who transferred them to his Villa Montalto. The name of this statue is inscribed on the front of the pedestal—

ΠΟΣΕΙΔΙΠΠΟΣ

This statue had an iron spike at the top of the head to support a *meniscus* or metal plate, the object of which was to protect the sculpture from injury of the weather in open air ; hence the origin of the *nimbus* or golden plates attached to the representation of saints in early paintings. Inscription very clear. The chair and costume are very similar to the Menander statue, but there is less dignity and self-possession in the bearing of this figure ; he seems somewhat bent with age. Like Menander, his feet are enveloped in thong sandals. The mask of this statue also had been detached by the insertion of the iron nail for the meniscus. These statues are supposed to have originally adorned the theatre at Athens, described by Pausanias.

Engraved in Mus. Pio Clem. vol. iii. tav. 16 ; Bouillon, vol. ii. pl. 25 ; Pistolesi, vol. v. tav. 45 ; Bunsen, vol. ii. p. 170 ; Visc. Icon. Grecque ; Clarac, Musée, pl. 841, No. 2120 ; Mus. Nap. No. 77. Musée Français. (See Portrait Gallery, No. 31.)

Dimensions : Height, 4′· 5″· 5.

292. BOAR (APER CALYDONIUS).

Engraved in Gori, Mus. Flor. Statue, tav. 69.

293. MELEAGER OF THE VATICAN.

Statue, life-size, of grey Greek Marble. From the VATICAN. Removed thither by Clement XIV., from the Palazzo Pighini, or Picchini.

Found, according to Flaminio Vacca, near the Basilica of Caius and Lucius, but, according to Aldrovandi, in a vineyard, near the Tiber, beyond the Porta Portese, in the 16th century. It originally belonged to Fusconi, physician to Paul III. This statue is wonderfully perfect : only the left hand missing, which no one has ventured to restore. It originally held a spear, as the traces still remain on the pedestal. A few fingers of the other hand have been completed. At his right side is a dog, and on the left a boar's head, placed on a rock, all of which are antique, and determine the character of the figure. It was formerly called an Adonis. The execution of this statue is very good, but not proportionate to its great celebrity. Meleager, son of the Calydonian King Œneus, who had taken a part in the Argonautic expedition, slew the monstrous boar which had ravaged his father's country. The hero is here represented resting after his victory; the head of the animal is on one side, and his faithful dog sits on the other.

Engraved in Mus. Pio Clem. vol. ii. tav. 34; Bouillon, vol. ii. pl. 7; Maffei, tav. 55; Pistolesi, vol. iv. tav. 86; Clarac, Musée, pl. 805, No. 2021; Bunsen, vol. ii. part 2, p. 123; Mus. Nap. 117; Musée Français.

Dimensions: Height, 6′· 6″· 1·

294. QUOIT-PLAYER (Discobolos), in Repose.

Statue, life-size, of Pentelic Marble. From the Vatican, where it had been placed by Pius VI. Found about eight miles from Rome, at Colambaro on the Via Appia, where Gallienus is supposed to have had a villa.

This statue is conjectured to be the work of the Argive sculptor Naucydes, mentioned by Pliny in his 34th Book. Few antiques have suffered so little injury as this: it has no fracture, but the surface of the body is corroded by the action of the damp. Tenons had been inserted in the marble and remain undisturbed. Were it not that the statue in many parts remains unfinished, we might fairly conclude this to be the actual *chef d'œuvre* of Naucydes, such is its superlative excellence. The *discus* is, exactly as described by Lucian, without aperture, handle or loop (Anacharsis seu de Gymn.): it is also seen in a painting from Stabiæ, Pitt Erc. vol. iii. tav. 25. A similar statue exists in England, with the right hand restored, quite open. The trunk is of a palm-tree with clusters of fruit. It belonged to Mr. Lock in the time of Cavaceppi, vol. i. pl. 42, and came from Villa Montalto. (*See* a note at p. 132 of Mus. Pio Clem. vol. iii.) Another in the Borghese, naked and erect This young Athlete holds the *discus* or quoit in his left hand: he seems to be marking the distance he has to throw. The band round his head is the crown usually worn by the victors.

Engraved in Mus. Pio Clem. vol. iii. tav. 26; Bouillon, vol. ii. pl. 17; Pistolesi, vol. vi. tav. 9; Annales du Musée; Clarac, Musée, pl. 862, No. 2194c; Bunsen, vol. ii. pt. 2, p. 242. Musée Français.

Dimensions: Height, 5′· 4″· 3·

295. FAUN (Satyr), snapping his Fingers.

Bronze Statue, life-size. From Naples. Found at Herculaneum, July, 1754.

The eyes of the original are filled with a vitreous paste of natural colours. Two glands hang on the neck, like on a goat; *askos*, upon a lion's skin.

Engraved in Mus. Bor. vol. ii. tav. 21; Clarac, Musée, pl. 719, No. 1720; compare a similar statue, Mus. Pio Clem. vol. i. tav. 47; Pistolesi, vol. v. 42; also at Munich, Glyptothek, No. 102.

296. ADONIS.

297. POLYMNIA.

Statue life-size, of Greek Marble. From the Louvre. Previously in the Borghese Collection at Rome.

The greater part of this statue is modern, having been excellently restored by Penna, a Roman sculptor. The portions of antique drapery that remain are of superlative excellence.

Engraved in Bouillon, vol. iii. pl. 11; Villa Borghese, st. 7, No. 12; Cl. Cat. 131, No. 306; Clarac, Musée, pl. 327, No. 1083. Musée Royal, vol. ii.
Dimensions: Height,

298. APOLLO SAUROCTONOS (THE LIZARD-KILLER).

From the VATICAN.

Discovered by Gavin Hamilton in 1777, on the Palatine Hill, among the foundations of the Villa Magnani, where Augustus is said to have had a residence. The marble is remarkably pure and beautiful. A repetition more injured was found at the same time.

Restorations: The right arm from above the elbow, left hand, part of face, and front of neck. The tree stem and lizard excepting the tail, left leg from below knee, and right leg from half way down the thigh.
Engraved in Mus. Pio Clem. vol. i. tav. 13; Pistolesi, vol. 6, tav. 11; Winckelmann, Mon. Ined. No. 40; Clarac, Musée, pl. 475, No. 905A; Bunsen, vol. ii. part 2, p. 243.

299. ATHLETE, OR BOXER.

Standing Figure with Raised Arms, bound in cestus. From the Collection at AROLSEN.

Probably from a bronze much restored. Very weak. The *cestus*, or *himantes* (ἱμαντες), were thongs bound round the hands and arms of the boxers to strengthen the blow. The cestus was used in very early times, and is often represented in ancient art.

Dimensions: Height, 5′· 1″· 5.

300. THE CLAPPING FAUN (SATYR).

Statue, life-size. From FLORENCE.

Pronounced by Mengs as flabby and inflated. The flesh has certainly that character, and indicates a satyr at a very different period of life from what we see represented in the *Periboetos* or *Anapauomenos*, Nos. 10 and 12. The instrument under his foot was called a *scabellum*; it is seen in various bacchanal sculptures, and under the foot of a female statue in the Capitol, Museum Capitolinum, vol. iii. tav. 36. Also in statue No. 303.

Restorations: The head and arms, by Michel Angelo Buonarotti.
Engraved in Gall. di Firenze; Maffei, tav. 35; Clarac, Musée, pl. 715, No. 1709; Wicar, Galerie de Florence, vol. iv. Musée Royal, vol. ii.
Dimensions: Height, 4′· 8″· 6·

301. APOLLO SAUROCTONOS (THE LIZARD-KILLER.)

A Statue of Parian Marble, small life. From the LOUVRE. Formerly in the Borghese Collection.

Restorations: The entire right hand from above the wrist. This Borghese one, with a repetition also in the same collection, are mentioned by Visconti, in text, vol. i. p. 131.
Engraved in Bouillon, vol. i. pl. 19; Villa Borghese, st. ii. No. 5; Cl. Cat. p. 10, No. 19; Clarac, Musée, pl. 267, No. 905. Musée Royal, vol. ii.
Dimensions: Height,

302. AMAZON.

Heroic size Statue of Grechetto Marble. From the VATICAN. The original was formerly in the Villa Mattei, on the Cælian hill, at Rome.

It was placed by Clement XIV. in the Vatican Museum. Perhaps the Amazon of Polycletus (Visconti, text, p. 269). See Pliny's story of the five Amazons made to adorn the temple of Ephesus (Hist. Nat. lib. xxxiv. c. 19). The statue is in the act of loosening her bow, the right arm raised over the head; a quiver is suspended at her left side, and a helmet lies at her left foot. The *pelta lunata*, a light shield of peculiar shape, and the *bipennis*, or double axe, are attached to the trunk on the other side; her tunic is high girt, and executed with much elegance; the fine small lines of the folds afford a greater contrast to the breadth and fulness of the limbs. The inscription on the horizontal surface of the plinth, TRANSLATA DE SCHOLA MEDICORVM, although Gerhard will not vouch for its genuineness, informs us that the statue was formerly placed in the portico built by Augustus for the use of medical practitioners. The place where it was found in modern times is not recorded. A repetition is in the Capitol, and placed there by Benedict XIV., 1753 (Mori, vol. ii. Sala Grande, tav. 22). Compare a Wounded Amazon statue with less drapery and no quiver (Pistolesi, vol. iv. tav. 15); and another in the Capitol (Mus. Capit. vol. iii. tav. 46; Mori, vol. ii. Sala Grande, tav. 21). They both have a peculiar piece of drapery round the neck; so also the Richelieu one in the Louvre. A similar statue at Petworth (Clarac, Musée, pl. 808, No. 203).

The AMAZONS were a race of warlike females, said to have come from the Caucasus, and to have settled about the river Thermodon, in Asia Minor, where they founded the city Themiscyra. Their queen was Hippolyte, and to obtain her girdle was one of the labours of Hercules. The Amazons invaded Attica in the reign of Theseus, and went with their queen, Penthesilea, to assist the Trojans. She was slain by Achilles.

Restorations: The arms.

Engraved in Bouillon, vol. ii. pl. 10; Maffei, tav. 109; Mus. Pio, Clem. vol. ii. tav. 38; Pistolesi, vol. iv. tav. 20; Clarac, Musée, pl. 811, No. 2031; Bunsen, vol. ii. part 2, p. 168; Musée Français.

Dimensions: Height of figure, 6′· 2″·3·; to top of hand, 6′· 3″ 0·

303. FAUN (SATYR), LIKE CLAPPING FAUN.

From PARIS.

Restored with syrinx in right hand, and holding a branch of support-stem in the other. Bellows under right foot.

304. WRESTLERS (PANCRATIASTÆ).

From FLORENCE.

The group is, in the opinion of some, connected with the Niobe family. One version of the fable says that the vengeance of Apollo and Diana came upon them, whilst the sons were exercising in the plain—the elder with their horses, the younger at wrestling. Moreover, Flaminio Vacca says that this group was disinterred at the same time, and in the same place, with the Niobe statues—namely, a little beyond the gate of S. Giovanni. They were purchased by the Grand Duke Ferdinand of Tuscany, who placed them in his garden on the Pincian Hill (Flaminio Vacca, Memorie, No. 79, p. 247). Flaxman (p. 96) calls them a fine example of anatomical study in difficult but harmonious composition. The Medici family paid 1800 crowns for this group when first found, a sum equal to 2000*l.* of our money at the present day (Flaxman, p. 23). They are properly called Pancratiastæ (Παγκρατιασται) from παγκρατιον, which strictly means a *complete contest*,—hence an exercise of the Greek youths, which combined both wrestling (παλη) and boxing (πυγμη). Athletæ (αθληται) were persons who contended for prizes (αθλα), and made it a profession. These boys are not even to be called Palæstæ (παλαισται) because throwing decided, but with the Pancratiastæ, the chief wrestling took place on the ground. The passionless heads of these youths accord strangely with other figures of the same epoch. These statues belong to a late period of Greek art, and we may expect the same amount of animation of countenance with the Niobid figures, or the statues of Scopas and Apollodorus. The heads are, in fact, not antique, which is proved by an old engraving, representing them in their original condition as when first discovered (Meyer, taf. 14 A). They may have been executed after the famous *symplegma* of Cephisodotus, son of Praxiteles, mentioned by Pliny, 36, cap. v. page 302. Sillig.

Restorations: Both heads, the left arm of uppermost figure, his left foot, right leg from the knee. Lower figure: right arm and right leg from above the knee.

Engraved, in the condition in which found, in pl. 109 of Insigniores Statuarum Romæ Icones; also in Meyer, taf. 1 A; Galleria di Fir. vol. iii. pl. 121; Meyer, taf. 14 A; Maffei, tav. 29; Gori, Mus. Flor. tav. 73; Clarac, Musée, pl. 858 A, No. 2176; Wicar, Galerie de Florence, vol. ii.

Dimensions: Height, 2′· 10″· 4·; Length, 3′· 11″· 0·

305. YOUNG FAUN (SATYR), CARRYING THE INFANT BACCHUS (DIONYSOS) ON HIS SHOULDERS.

He plays cymbals. A syrinx and pedum hang upon the vine-stump. Group in Greek Marble. From NAPLES. Formerly in the Farnesina at Rome; found in the Campagna di Roma.

Greek art. The only antique portion of the boy is the thighs, and parts of the figure attached to the shoulders of the faun. The face of the faun is modern. He has a tail. The extremities of the figure and part of the base also are restored. A similar statue with more of the child perfect in the Villa Albani. Clarac. Musée, pl. 704, B. No. 1628, B. The faun tripping on his toes carries the infant Bacchus on his right shoulder. The accessories seem to be ancient, and merit attention. The stem on the left bears vine-leaves and grapes. A pedum and syrinx are also attached.

Engraved in Mus. Bor. vol. ii. tav. 25; Clarac, Musée. pl. 704, B. No. 1628A; Neapels, p. 35, No. 103.

306. SILENUS, CARRYING THE INFANT BACCHUS (DIONYSOS).

Statue, Grechetto Marble. From the LOUVRE. Formerly in the Villa Borghese at Rome.

Discovered in the 16th century on the Quirinal, in the gardens of Sallust, together with the famous Borghese Vase (No. 352), a work that may rank with the Torso, Laocoon, the Nile, and many other chef d'œuvres. Most probably of Roman time (Glypt. p. 103). In the Vatican Chiaramonti group the trunk is covered with vine-leaves and clusters (Pistolesi, vol. iv. tav. 7). A statue also is in the Glyptothek at Munich, besides the Museo Chiaramonti one (Glypt. Cat. No. 115). Musée Royal, vol. i.

Restorations: The hands and half the right fore-arm, and the extremities of the right foot of Silenus. The left leg, left arm, and a portion of the right arm of the infant; also the trunk of tree as far as the *nebris* or fawn-skin.

Engraved in Cl. Cat. p. 257, No. 709; Clarac, Musée, pl. 333, No. 1556; Bouillon, pl. 54; Maffei, tav. 77; Villa Borghese, st. 9, No. 13.

Dimensions: Height, 6′· 1″· 4·

307. POSIDONIUS.

Sitting Statue, life-size, of Pentelic Marble. From the Louvre. Previously in the Borghese Collection.

Formerly called Belisarius. Identified by an inscribed bust in the Farnesina Collection. Left side of square block carved into folding chair. The general conception of this figure, both in its attitude and the arrangement of the drapery, is excellent, but the original execution has been destroyed in many parts, especially the face, by a modern chisel.

Restorations: The hand, fore arm, and a great portion of the feet are modern restorations; also many parts of the drapery.

Engraved in Bouillon, vol. ii. pl. 28; Clarac, Cat. p. 46, No. 89; Visconti, Icon. Gr. vol. i. pl. 24; Villa Borghese, St. 4, No. 4; Clarac, Musée, pl. 327, No. 2119. See Portrait Gallery, No. 33.

Dimensions: Height, 3′· 10″· 6·

308. DEMOSTHENES.

A Sitting Statue, life-size, of Pentelic Marble. From the Louvre. Formerly in the Vatican, whither it had been transported by Pius VI. from the gardens of Pope Sixtus V. in the Villa Negroni or Montalto. The head did not originally belong to this statue, although antique. Bought by Jenkins. Covered with a simple mantle or pallium, he opens the roll upon his knees, and seems to meditate profoundly.

Restorations: The right hand and part of the fore-arm, the entire left arm and drapery near it. The nose, left ear, portion of right leg, feet, and part of the neck.

Engraved in Visconti, Mus. Pio. Clem. vol. iii. tav. 14; Bouillon, vol. ii. pl. 22; Guatt. Mon. In., vol. iv. Giugno, tav. 1; Cl. Cat. No. 92; Clarac, Musée, pl. 283, No. 2099A; Mus. Nap. No. 72. See Portrait Gallery, No. 19.

Dimensions: Height, 4′· 7″· 9·

309. GLADIATOR, WOUNDED AND PROSTRATE.

Statue, life-size, of Luni Marble. From the Capitol, at Rome, whither it was transferred by Clement XII. from the Villa Ludovisi. Found among the ruins of the gardens of Sallust—the Hand-book to Rome says at Antium —in 1770.

Mr. James Yates has recently published a learned essay upon this figure, of which the following is the substance. The statue was made in Italy, under the early emperors, perhaps Hadrian. It represents a native of one of the northern nations opposed to the Romans, either Gauls, Germans, Dacians, Goths, or others. He was a man of some rank in his native army, perhaps the *Cornian*, or blower of the horn as signal for battle, which instrument lies on the ground. Having been taken captive, he has been condemned to be trained by the Lanista, and is supposed to be expiring in the arena, thinking of his home and country, as described by Lord Byron. This statue was found together with the so-called Paetus and Arria, still in the Villa Ludovisi; and they most probably formed part of the ornaments of some vast Roman monument commemorating a victory over barbarians. "The surface of the Dying Gladiator seems rubbed so as to give an extra polish. There is a want of sharpness, precision, and fulness about the forms. His ears are almost lost, but the bottom of one is clearly traceable, although it much resembles a lock of hair."—MS. Journal, Rome, April 25th, 1844. He wears a gold-twisted ornament called a torque round his neck. This was a sign of wealth and rank among foreign nations, and is also seen on the sarcophagus, No. 125, in the Bas-relief gallery.

"The 'dying gladiator' is one of those masterpieces of antiquity which exhibits a knowledge of anatomy and of man's nature. He is not resting; he is not falling; but in the position of one wounded in the chest and seeking relief in that anxious and oppressed breathing which attends a mortal wound with loss of blood. He seeks support to his arms, not to rest them or to sustain the body, but to fix them that their action may be transferred to the chest, and thus assist the labouring respiration. The nature of his sufferings leads to this attitude. In a man expiring from loss of blood, as the vital stream flows, the heart and lungs have the same painful feeling of want, which is produced by obstruction to the breathing. As the blood is draining from him he pants and looks wild, and the chest heaves convulsively. And so the ancient artist has placed this statue in the posture of one who suffers the extremity of difficult respiration."—SIR CHARLES BELL, *Anatomy of Expression*, p. 194.

Restorations: The entire right arm, the extremities of the feet, and part of the plinth.

Engraved in Mus. Cap. vol. iii. tav. 67; Bouillon, vol. ii. pl. 20; Maffei, tav. 65; Righetti; Mori, vol. ii. Sala Grande, tav. 31; Bunsen, vol. iii. p. 248; Clarac, Musée, pl. 869, No. 2214; Mr. Yates's Memoir to the Archæological Institute at Bristol, 1853. Musée Français.

Dimensions: Height, 2′· 9″· 0; Length, 5′· 5″· 9·

310. ACHILLES.

Heroic Statue of Parian Marble. From the LOUVRE. Previously in the Borghese Collection at Rome.

A ring above the right ancle. The workmanship of the knees and thighs is remarkably excellent, but the body is hard and swollen in parts. The right arm looks well in front, but viewed sideways, is heavy and incorrect. The features want grandeur of treatment.

Restorations: The left fore-arm, fingers of right hand, and the tips of some of the toes.

Engraved in Bouillon, vol. ii. pl. 14; Villa Borghese, st. 1, No. 9; Cl. Cat., p. 68, No. 144; Hirt. B. B., tab. 7, No. 2; Clarac, Cat., pl. 263, No. 2073.

Dimensions: Height, 6′· 11″· 6·

311. BACCHUS.

Statue, life-size. From Naples.

Raising the right hand with a bunch of grapes, and holding a *cantharus* in the left. The stem on that side ornamented with vines.

Engraved in Clarac, Musée, pl. 659, No. 1586; Mus. Bor. t. 1, No. 120.

312. GERMANICUS.

Statue, life-size, of Parian Marble. From the Louvre. Placed by Louis XIV. at Versailles, and previously in the Villa Negroni at Rome.

On the shell of the tortoise, beneath the drapery is the following Greek inscription;

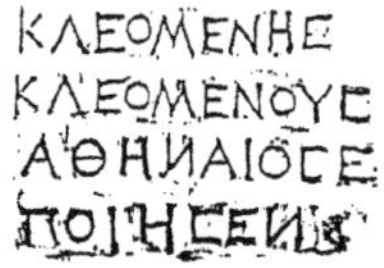

The forms of the letters are remarkable. The inscription in this cast is unfortunately illegible. Hitherto this figure has been called Germanicus, son of Drusus and Antonia, the niece of Augustus. From the peculiarity of countenance, and arrangement of the hair, it is the portrait of a somewhat aged Roman personage; not Germanicus certainly, because he died in the 34th year of his age, and the features do not at all correspond with his portrait on ancient coins. The attitude is that of a Mercury; his left hand originally held a caduceus; and the chlamys upon the left shoulder, which might have appeared to be kept from further falling by the upper part of the caduceus, and the tortoise below, are only further indications of the god of eloquence.

Restorations: The thumb and fore-finger of the left hand.

Engraved in Bouillon, vol. ii. pl. 36; Maffei, tav. 69; Cl. Cat. p. 259, No. 712; Clarac, Musée, pl. 318, No. 2314; Mus. Nap. No. 83. Musée Français. See Portrait Gallery, No. 115.

Dimensions: Height, 5′. 11″· 0·

313. ADONIS, or APOLLO, of Capua.

Statue heroic size, of Grechetto Marble. Fom Naples.

Found in the Amphitheatre, at Capua. The head, very like that of an Erôs, is turned to the left, as if listening. Gerhard considers the figure to have been somewhat overrated. It belongs to the age of Hadrian.

Restorations: Part of the thighs and legs, the trunk of tree, with bow and quiver, the right hand and left arm,—by the modern sculptor, Cali.

Engraved in Mus. Bor. vol. ii. tav. 24; Clarac, Musée, pl. 484, No. 932, pl. 650, No. 1492; Neapels, p. 87, No. 287.

Dimensions: Height, 7′· 3″· 5·

314. ANTINOUS, as a Good Genius (Agathodaimon).

Statue, heroic size, of Parian Marble. From Berlin. Formerly at Sans Souci. It belonged to Cavaceppi.

The hands and feet of this figure are antique and remarkably fine. One finger of the right hand has been replaced. It is altogether wonderfully preserved. The eyes are hollowed to receive glass or stones. The serpent, as the emblem of the good genius, occurs on coins of Nero struck at Alexandria. Νεος ἀγαθος δαιμων. The elephant's trunk and serpent seem to bear a reference to the Indian Bacchus, and therefore Visconti prefers to call it Antinous-Bacchus, rather than Agathodaimon. See a little double Hermes, No. 385. Levezow says, page 82, that the statue is of Luni marble.

Engraved in Bouillon, vol. ii. pl. 51; Berlin Cat. No. 264, p. 24; Levezow, über Antinous, tav. 6; Cavaceppi, vol. i. No. 24; Mus. Nap. No. 194; Musée Royal, vol. i.

Dimensions: Height,

315. DISCOBOLUS.

This cast is much distorted.

316. MERCURY (Hermês).

Statue of Parian Marble. From the Vatican. Found in the pontificate of Paul III., at Rome, upon the Esquiline, near S. Martino dei Monti, in a spot formerly called Adrianello.

Placed by Paul III. in the Belvedere of his palace; it was known by the name of the Antinous of the Vatican. Not superior to the Jason or Germanicus. A similar statue is in the possession of Lord Lansdowne, with the bent arm perfect. A repetition exists in Munich (Glyptothek, No. 127). Visconti was the first to consider it a Mercury. Very probably a Meleager, and in this opinion Winckelmann concurs. The right arm and left hand are modern. Gerhard says, although the head bears resemblance to the favourite of Hadrian, the style of art bespeaks an earlier and superior time. The probability of this statue being a Mercury rests upon the shortness of the hair, naturally curling, the delicacy of the form, and a slight inclination of the head. Visconti regards the light *chlamys* which enfolds the right arm as symbolical of his readiness to execute the commands of the gods. It is true that we neither see the *petasus*, *caduceus*, purse, or *talaria*, but they are not absolutely essential to identify the son of Maia. The style of head, character of the limbs, and general attitude would suffice. But a statue of Mercury, with caduceus and winged feet, and in precisely the same attitude, existed in the Farnese Palace, at Rome. A statue formerly at Versailles, and now in the Louvre, is also quite similar (engraved in vol. i. pl. 26, of Bouillon): it is of mediocre workmanship, but the attitude and peculiar throw of the *chlamys* round the arm, together with the short round curls of the hair, accord with the statue of the Belvedere. In addition, there are unequivocal remains of the wings to the head of the Versailles figure, and a fragment of the caduceus remained in his left hand. Compare No. 287 for the same figure restored. The origin in the Vatican remains as in the statue before us.

Engraved in Mus. Pio Clem. vol. i. tav. 7; Bouillon, pl. 27; Bunsen, vol. ii. p. 141; Pistolesi, vol. iv. tav. 97; Maffei, tav. 3; Clarac, Musée, pl. 665, No. 1514; Bunsen, vol. ii. part 2, p. 141; Mus. Nap. No. 129; Musée Français.

Dimensions: Height, 6′· 7″· 8·

317. HERCULES (Heraklês) (Reposing).

Colossal Statue of Grechetto Marble. The work of Glycon. From Naples. Formerly in the Farnese Collection at Rome.

Commonly called the Farnese Hercules. Found in the baths of Caracalla, at Rome. The accounts, however, of the discovery of this statue vary in the most extraordinary manner. Inscribed—

ΓΛΥΚΩΝ
ΑΘΗΝΑΙΟϹ
ЄΠΟΙЄΙ

The work is well preserved. "There is a joint visible in the statue above the knees, which passes in the left knee directly through the ligament under the patella; the same in the other leg, but it slopes upwards and outwards, almost bounding the tendon of the vastus externus. The toes have been restored in plaster. Inscription is cut in thin sharp letters" (MS. Journal, Naples, April 20th, 1844). Mengs (vol. ii. p. 21) suspects, from the silence of Fulvio Orsini and Flaminio Vacca respecting the inscription, that it has been added since the discovery of the statue. Flaxman says (page 229): "The Hercules Farnese was evidently one of the first favourites of antiquity, from its frequent repetition in bronze and marble, on gems, and coins. It is worthy of remark that some statues of Hercules, in the same attitude of repose with that surnamed Farnese, but of much earlier date, have the proportions of common men, and that a series of them may be found in various collections, gradually increasing to the terrific strength of Glycon's statue. The head of this formidable hero bears a noble resemblance to his father Jupiter. The anatomical detail in the body and limbs is more distinct than in any other work of antiquity."

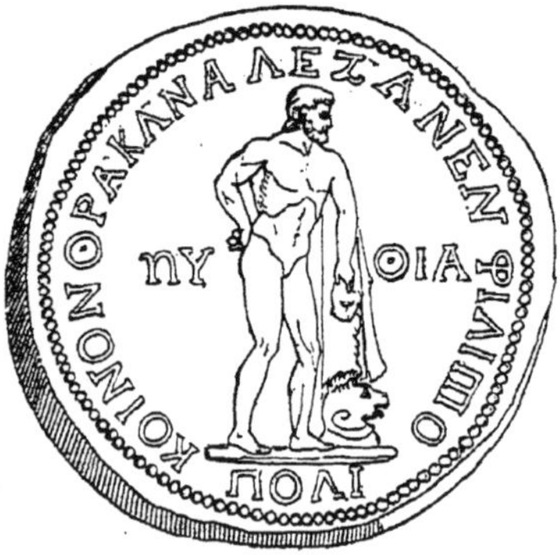

Coin of Caracalla, struck at Philippopolis, in Thrace, showing the statue of the reposing Hercules.

This statue is represented on the reverse of a coin of Caracalla, struck at Corinth, inscribed CLI. COR., now in the British Museum, and on another coin of the same emperor struck at Philippopolis in Thrace.

Restorations: Half the left fore-arm, and the hand, also the toes of both feet. The head and extremities were much broken. The right hand holding the apples is ancient. The legs, which were not found at first were supplied by Guglielmo della Porta, until 1787.

Engraved in Mus. Bor. vol. iii. tav. 24; Maffei, tav. 49; Clarac, Musée, pl. 789, No. 1978; Neapels, p. 31, No. 97.

Dimensions: Height,

318 and 319. DIOSCURI.

CASTOR AND POLLUX. THE COLOSSI OF MONTE CAVALLO.

These stupendous groups were found in the baths of Constantine on the Quirinal Hill, now called Monte Cavallo. Flaminius Vacca relates a tradition that Constantine had brought them to this spot from the vestibule of the palace of Nero, and that many architectural fragments, found together with the figures, confirm this opinion. Visconti believes them to be copies made at Rome in the time of Nero, from bronze statues of considerable celebrity. They have never been thoroughly finished, many masses upon them remain imperfect, and the same also is the case in the colossal figures of the Nile and Tiber found at the same time. Flaxman says (p. 94): "We may fairly presume the colossal statues on Monte Cavallo, in Rome, to be the works of Phidias and Praxiteles, as inscribed on their pedestals, because the animated character and style of sculpture seem peculiar to the age in which those artists lived; and because in the frieze of the Parthenon there is a young hero governing a horse, which bears so strong a resemblance to those groups, that it would be difficult to believe it was not a first idea for them by one of those artists."

I have already expressed my conviction (in the Introduction, page 42 of Greek Court) that these statues are copies from bronze originals belonging to the Macedonian epoch. The rising and snaky hair on the forehead, and exaggerated expression of the eyes and mouth, have also a strong affinity to the age of Alexander. The surface of the flesh is very much corroded, but in some parts where it has been protected, as, for instance, down the cheek of the left-hand figure, we observe that it has been elaborately finished. The warts or mammiform

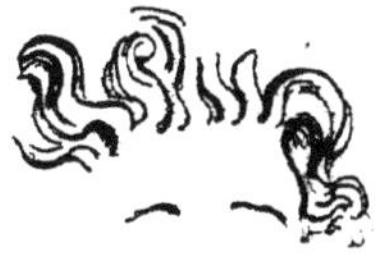

projections on various parts of this figure are very remarkable. There is a grand massiveness about the limbs and trunk in both groups. The arms and legs taper remarkably towards the extremities, and the hands appear very small in proportion. The drapery folding round the arm of the right-hand figure is wrought in the true grand style. The hollows and grooving of the folds are wonderfully executed. It is worthy of the statutes in the Parthenon pediment. The veins are delicately shown in several parts, and clearly to be traced inside one of the arms where the surface has been sheltered from the action of the weather. A vein is also traceable upon the shoulder muscle. In the open mouth of the right-hand figure the teeth are distinctly marked; the eye-balls also are strongly indicated by deep-cut lines, and the pupil hollowed out into a peculiar form. The eyelids are made more effective by very deep channelled lines above and below: this gives a surprising force of expression.

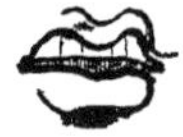

The eyeballs of the horses are also marked in the same manner, the centre or pupil being very deep. This expedient is not to be seen in any of the sculptures of the Parthenon, the projecting eyeball of the celebrated horse (No. 185, c.) is perfectly smooth, and the bronze horse, from Florence, also, Nos. 71 and 69. The cheeks of these horses are remarkably

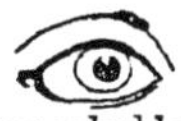

broad and the bones quite flat: there is great animation of expression about them. Their faces are traversed by veins, which show very strongly upon the bellies. The creases of the skin at the junction of the head with the throat are somewhat exaggerated. The breast-plate or *lorica* standing at the side of the figure does not accord with the formation of such armour at the time of Phidias. Neither upon the Parthenon nor upon the painted vases of the next period do we find such an arrangement of straps at the shoulders and round the hips; but we *do* find them in connection with statues of Alexander the Great, and used then on the ground for support also. Thus it is in the famous statue of Alexander, found at Gabii, and in the Rondanini Alexander, now at Munich. The celebrated equestrian bronze of Alexander, found at Herculaneum, has a somewhat similar style of armour. In that group the eyeballs of the hero and his charger are deeply pierced. Whatever the exact epoch of these Monte Cavallo figures may be, there can be no doubt that they belong to a very superior class of art, admitting of comparison, for grandeur of style and conception, with the well-ascertained works of Phidias in the pediments of the Parthenon. These statues occupy a prominent position at Rome on the ancient Quirinal hill, which is now called, from these groups, *Monte Cavallo*. They stand in front of the Pope's Palace. The names of Phidias and Praxiteles are inscribed in modern Italian letters upon the pedestals, but not traceable further back than the time of Sixtus V.

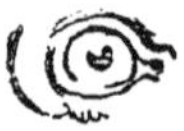

Engraved in Meyer, taf. 15, figs. A and B; Maffei, tav. 11 to 13; old engraving, by Bunsen, vol. iii. part 2, p. 404; Clarac, Musée, pl. 812 A; No. 2043; referred to in Mus. Pio Clem. vol. i. p. 288, note (2).

319. VACANT.

320. MONUMENT OF LYSICRATES.

Choragic Monument at Athens, erected, according to the inscription on it at the time that Evanetus was Archon, B.C. 335-4, whilst Alexander the Great was invading Persia. The entire height is thirty-four feet. It is circular, and the diameter eight feet. Upon the upper part of the wall, between each of the columns, are two tripods in low relief. The roof elegantly tends to a summit upon which a bronze tripod originally stood. It was customary for those who obtained the tripods as prizes in musical contests to dedicate them in some temple, or in separate buildings erected for them along a street on the east side of the Acropolis, which obtained the name of the street of the tripods. This monument is the earliest known instance of Corinthian architecture, the capitals of the columns are very beautiful, and the shafts are fluted in a peculiar manner. The frieze is ornamented with figures illustrative of the adventures of Bacchus and the Etruscan pirates, narrated in the hymns of Homer. Bacchus was seized sleeping by pirates and conveyed on board their ship; he punished them by converting the ship into a vine and the pilot into a raging lion. As the mariners leapt into the sea, they were changed into dolphins. This transformation is represented on the frieze. Satyrs appear also punishing the snake-bound Etruscans with fire. These sculptures are valuable examples of the age of Lysippus. The monument was only used as a pedestal for the tripod belonging to Lysicrates, but in later times when a monastery was built around it, the interior was converted into a sanctum for the Prior. A view of the interior may be seen in Dodwell's Travels (vol. i. p. 289).

Engraved in Stuart's Antiquities of Athens, vol. i. pl. 24.

321. DEMOSTHENES.

Standing Figure, life-size, of Greek Marble. From the VATICAN.

A scrinium at his feet. Standing statue, life-size, bare-breasted, with mantle thrown over the left shoulder.

Restorations: The hands and the scroll.

Engraved in Clarac, Musée, pl. 842, No. 2122; Pistolesi, vol. iv. tav. 19; Bunsen, vol. ii. part 2, p. 94.

See Portrait Gallery, No. 19.

Dimensions: Height, 6′· 5″· 2.

322. SOPHOCLES.

Standing Statue, life-size. From the LATERAN MUSEUM, at ROME. Found at Terracina, and presented by Cardinal Antonelli.

A remarkably fine figure, and very similar in attitude and costume to the statue of Æschines, No. 326. H.B. last ed. p. 204. The round box at his right side serves as a *bookcase.* It contains 8 papyri, viz., rolls or books (for binding was unknown in those days), and this affords us a very interesting opportunity of observing the different ways in which they might be arranged. Sometimes they were rolled up entirely—sometimes from both ends; the latter when they were only half read through, as persons were compelled to unroll as they read. The lines of writing, however, did not continue the whole length of the sheet, but were broken into columns as our newspapers and dictionaries.—(See, for further illustration, p.p. 20 and 50 of Pompeian Court Catalogue.) The statue of Demosthenes, No. 308, has also a *scrinium*, or bookcase; but it is closed, and does not afford us the same curious particulars.

Dimensions: Height,

323. VACANT.

324. PHOCION.

Statue, life-size, of Pentelic Marble. From the VATICAN. Found at Rome, among the foundations of the Palazzo Gentili.

Altogether a fine work. Statue of a warrior wearing the *chlamys*, a simple cloak, and helmet. Visconti saw a similarity between the workmanship of this figure, and that of the Demosthenes now in England at Knowle. Visconti afterwards thought it might be one of the seven chiefs against Thebes. The legs are modern and fairly restored, so also the left hand. No doubt the portrait of an ancient Greek, but we have little evidence of its being the actual portrait of Phocion (Mus. Pio Clem. text, p. 310). Standing with bare feet, a helmet on head, and the body enveloped in a thick mantle, or *chlamys.* The ideal beauty of this figure renders it much more probable to have been one of the heroes of the ancient games, perhaps one of the founders, Adrastus or Amphiaraus. A small repetition also in the Vatican.

Engraved in Mus. Pio Clem. vol. ii. tav. 43; Bouillon, vol. ii. pl. 23; Pistolesi, vol. vi. tav. 10; Bunsen, vol. ii. part 2, p. 242; Mus. Nap. No. 75; Pistolesi, vol. vi. tav. 59; Clarac, Musée, pl. 842, No. 2117; Musée Française.

See Portrait Gallery, No. 23.

Dimensions: Height, 6′· 11″· 4.

325. VACANT.

326. ARISTIDES, OR ÆSCHINES.

Statue, life-size, of Greek Marble. From NAPLES. Found in Herculaneum.

This portrait is rather, from the general appearance, to be ranked among philosophers than statesmen, and is remarkably like a statue of Marcus Aurelius at Venice, engraved in Ferrarius, p. 145, and Zanetti, Stat. di S. Marco, vol. i. No. 27. This statue was found in the Villa of the Papyri, at Herculaneum : the name of an orator or a literary man would therefore be much more appropriate than Aristides, whose portrait has never yet been satisfactorily ascertained.

Engraved in Mus. Bor. vol. i. tav. 50; Clarac, Musée, pl. 843, No. 2136; Mus. Bor. No. 2136; Neapels, p. 105, No. 363; H. B. p. 169.

See Portrait Gallery, No. 8.

Dimensions : Height, 6′·6″·4.

327. PHILOSOPHER, KNOWN BY THE NAME OF ZENO.

Statue, life-size, of Grechetto Marble. From the CAPITOL.

Found in 1701, near Lanuvium, the modern Civita Lavinia, where Marcus Aurelius had a villa. In the same spot, and at the same time, was discovered the beautiful faun called περιβοητος (No. 12). A similar statue at Munich (Glypt. Cat. No. 162). The square mantle, or *pallium*, which envelopes the figure, the cut of his beard, and style of hair, and the *scrinium*, or box for rolls at his feet, show him to be a philosopher.

Restorations : The right arm and the feet.

Engraved in Mus. Cap.; Bouillon, vol. ii. pl. 20; Visc. Icon. Grecque; Bunsen; Mus. Nap. No. 71.

See Portrait Gallery, No. 21.

Dimensions : Height, 5′·7″·4.

328. MINERVA (ATHÊNÊ).

Colossal Bust of Pentelic Marble. From MUNICH. Formerly in the Albani Collection.

A portion of a statue exactly like the Minerva of Velletri (No. 351), only far superior in execution. The eyes were hollow to receive coloured stones, and very probably both have been copied from a Phidiac original, which, to judge from the execution of this and other repetitions, must have been a bronze, perhaps the Lemnian Minerva which stood on the Acropolis at Athens (see p. 29 of Introduction to Greek Court). The eye-sockets have been filled up, and the plates of the helmet, the nose, part of the under-lip, and some of the snakes of the Ægis, are modern restorations. It was found in the ruins of the villa of Licinius Murena, near Tusculum. Instead of the usual plume or crest at the top of the helmet is placed a serpent. The hair is gathered behind in a mass and falls down the neck, in the manner called by the Greeks παραπεπλεγμενη (—ως, Liddle and Scott).

Engraved in Millin. Mon. Ant. Ined. ii. 24; Bouillon, vol. i. pl. 70; Glyptothek Cat. No. 84.

329. MELPOMENE.

A Colossal Bust of fine-grained Parian Marble. From the VATICAN. Found at the entrance of the Theatre in Hadrian's Villa, at Tivoli.

The hair is arranged like that of a tragic mask.

Visconti, Mus. Pio Clem. vol. vi. tav. 10.

330. YOUNG JUPITER.

A colossal Head. Very fine. From NAPLES.

331. LUCIUS VERUS.

Colossal Head. See Portrait Gallery, No. 50.

332. PLOTINA.

Colossal Head. See Portrait Gallery, No. 99.

333. LUCIUS VERUS.

334. JULIA DOMNA PIA.

Colossal Head. See Portrait Gallery, No. 94.*

335. JUNO.

From Ludovisi Collection at Rome.

336. MEDUSA HEAD, FROM COLOGNE.

From COLOGNE. In the Museum bequeathed by Prof. Wallraff to his native city. Very little of the sculpture is really antique. Compare the Medusa mask from Munich, No. 410.

337. OLYMPIAN JUPITER (ZEUS).

Colossal Bust of Italian Marble. From the VATICAN. Found at Otriculum during the excavations carried on by Pius VI.

The largest and finest head known of this divinity. No other representation of the countenance of the chief of gods and men can be compared with this sublime work of art. It accords more completely with the description of Homer and the statue of Phidias than any other. Benignity, serenity, power, and majesty, seem all united in this magnificent head. What then must have been the glory of the entire statue of which this only formed a part?

Restorations: The head-band, back of the head, and neck.

Engraved in Bouillon, vol. i. pl. 65; Mus. Pio Clem. vol. vi. tav. 1; Pistolesi, vol. v. tav. 103; Bunsen, vol. ii. part 2, page 225; Mus. Nap. No. 116. Musée Français.

338. TITUS VESPASIAN.

Colossal Bust of Greek Marble. From NAPLES. Formerly in the Farnese Collection.

See Portrait Gallery, No. 39.

Engraved in Mus. Bor. vol. xiii. tav. 24.

339. JUPITER SERAPIS, WITH MODIUS AND RAYS.

Bust, colossal, of Pentelic Marble. From the VATICAN. Found on the Via Appia, at a place called Colombaro, in the same excavation as the Discobolus, No. 294.

Serapis was an ancient Egyptian divinity who presided over the dead. His worship increased at the time of the foundation of Alexandria, and Ptolemy the first was impelled by a dream to bring to Egypt an old statue of the Infernal Jupiter from Sinope, which was soon associated with Serapis by the Egyptians. The emblems of Pluto and the earlier Serapis were thus united and introduced into Rome as one divinity. The age of Hadrian seems to have been the most productive of images of this kind, and of a very superior style of art. The Egyptian Goddess Isis was introduced into Rome about the same time as Serapis. The execution of this bust falls very short of the grand conception and invention of the character.

Restorations : The nose and a portion of the left shoulder. The seven spikes to represent rays are modern, but the holes in the marble and representation on coins clearly prove them to have formerly existed.

Engraved in Mus. Pio Clem. vol. vi. tav. 15 ; Pistolesi, vol. v. tav. 110 ; Bouillon, vol. i. pl. 70 ; Bunsen, vol. ii. part 2, page 226 ; Mus. Nap. No. 7.

340. MARINE DEITY—OCEANUS, OR, MORE PROBABLY, TRITON.

Terminal Bust of Hermes, of Grechetto Marble. From the VATICAN. Found near Pozzuoli, by Gavin Hamilton, who ceded it to Clement XIV. for his museum.

Crowned with vine-leaves and grapes, with two horns at the top of his head, scales or vine-leaves over his countenance and breast. Two dolphins are starting out of his beard, the hair of which, and of the head, also resembles flowing water. The front of this terminal bust is marked with undulations like waves.

Restorations : The nose and mouth.

Engraved in Bouillon, vol. i. pl. 65 ; Mus. Pio Clem. vol. vi. tav. 5 ; Pistolesi, vol. v. tav. 106 ; Bunsen, vol. ii. part 2, p. 225 ; Mus. Nap. No. 113. Compare a very similar bronze bust of a younger Triton in the British Museum, engraved in the Dilettanti Specimens, vol. i. pl. 55. Musée Français.

341. JUNO.

Colossal Head. Found at Carthage.

342. PERTINAX.

Colossal Head. See Portrait Gallery, No. 49.

343. TRAJAN.

Colossal Head. See Portrait Gallery, No. 45.

344. MARCUS AURELIUS.

Colossal Head. See Portrait Gallery, No. 48.

345. M. AGRIPPA.

See Portrait Gallery, No. 113.

346. THALIA.

Colossal Bust of fine-grained Parian Marble. From the VATICAN. Found at the entrance to the Theatre to Hadrian's Villa, at Tivoli.

The hair is adorned with vine, and arranged altogether like that of a mask. Visconti, Mus. Pio Clem. vol. vi. tav. 10.

347. ANTINOUS.

Colossal Bust of the Braschi Statue, of Carrara or Luni Marble. For the entire figure see page 14 of Introduction.

The entire statue, eleven feet high, is now in the Lateran Museum; it was formerly in the Palazzo Braschi at Rome. Found at the close of the last century by Gavin Hamilton, at Sta. Maria della Villa near Palestrina; it was put together by Pierantoni. Pope Pius VI. gave it to his nephew, Duke Braschi, from whose palace in the Piazza Navona it was removed to the Lateran.

Engraved in Levezow über Antinous, tav. 7 and 8; Guattani, per 1805, Genarro; Bunsen, vol. iii. part 3, p. 405. See Portrait Gallery, No. 79.

348. HEAD OF THE YOUTHFUL BACCHUS.

From the Museum at LEYDEN. Brought originally from Asia Minor.

It is in reality part of a statue; a broad band passes across the forehead, and causes a peculiar starting of the hair, above which, mingled with the ivy berries, it has a very singular effect.

Restorations: The nose, lips, and some portions of eyelids, part of hair also on each side of the head.

Engraved in Mon. dell' Inst. vol. iii. tav. 41, 1.

349. JUNO (HÊRÊ).

Colossal Head. Fom the VILLA LUDOVISI.

The most celebrated and grandest representation of the countenance of the Queen of the Gods. This enormous head is surmounted by a frontlet or tiara, adorned with palmettes and a row of beads, which hang down on each side of the neck.

Restoration: The tip of the nose.

Engraved in Meyer; Geschichte der Kunst. taf. 20; Bunsen, vol. iii. part 2, p. 582.

350. DIRCE, TIED TO A BULL; COMMONLY CALLED THE TORO FARNESE.

A colossal Group of Grechetto Marble. From NAPLES.

Formerly in the Farnese Collection, where it occupied the second court of the Farnese Palace, and ornamented a fountain. It was removed to Naples in 1786. For a long time this group was placed in the Villa Reale, and seen to great advantage in the open air, but it has since been united with the other masterpieces of sculpture in the Gallery of the Studij. It was found originally in the baths of Caracalla, with the Hercules, No. 317, during the pontificate of Paul III.

This celebrated group is especially interesting as one of the few works remaining to us which has been described by Pliny, xxxvi. 5-4. He tells us that it is the work of two Rhodian sculptors, Apollonius and Tauriscus, sons of Artemidorus, and carved in one block of marble. He further states that it was brought from Rhodes to Rome by Asinius Pollio in the age of Augustus.

There seems no reason for doubting that this is the very group mentioned by Pliny, and we may regard it as the best, if not the only example of that colossal style of sculpture which had its origin in the south of Asia Minor, and was perfected by Chares of Lindus. The infuriated bull is being restrained for a moment by the two sons of Antiope and Jupiter, whilst Dirce, their victim, lies almost prostrate on the ground, attempting to moderate the wrath of Amphion, who is distinguished by a lyre placed at his feet. Antiope stands behind, in so insulated a position that it is doubtful whether she belonged to the group originally. This wonderful composition is overloaded with accessories; it has been much restored, but that the general appearance has not undergone much change may be seen in two ancient representations upon coins here appended. Flaxman says (p. 95): "Zethus and Amphion, tying Dirce to the bull's horns, an example of filial vengeance for a persecuted mother, is as heroic in conception as vast in execution. The restorations of this group are so bad, that they become only tolerable by something like an assimilation of spirit in their union with the ancient and venerable fragments."

Restorations: All the figure of Dirce above the middle of the body, the head and neck of Amphion, both arms and part of the hands, the legs from the ankles to above the knee, three middle toes of left foot, are antique. Part of the chlamys on his shoulder has been restored. The entire head of Zethus, the left leg from foot to the attachment of thigh to the tree, the right knee and part of leg, the right arm between wrist and shoulder, and left fore-arm with drapery and the hand holding chords. Antiope, entire head and neck, right arm and hand, left arm and hand holding a lance, part also of the left leg. The bull has the ears, horns, fore-legs, and lower part of hind legs restored. The bacchanal boy seated, his right leg attached to the rock, the right fore-arm and hand and entire left arm to the wrist, together with a few restorations in the head, goat's skin, and tunic. The Dog, excepting a paw, is entirely modern. The sides of the base, which seem teeming with animal life, are more or less restored.

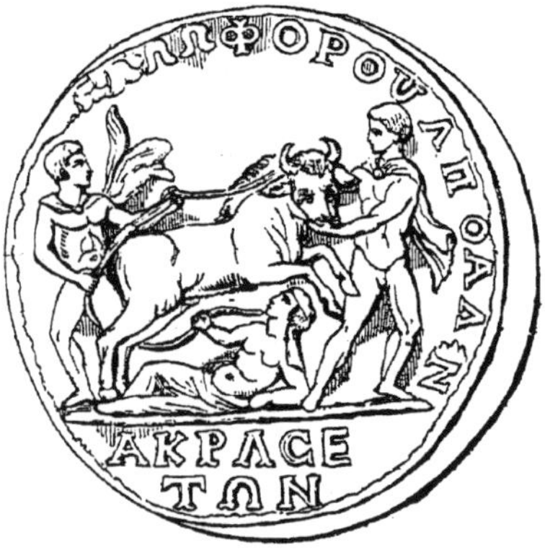

Coin of Alexander Severus, struck at Acrasus, in Lydia. From the Imperial Cabinet at Vienna.

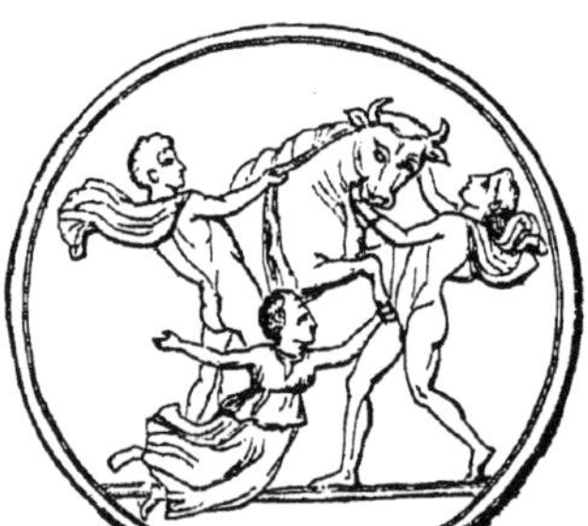

From a Contorniate Medal in the British Museum.

Dirce was the wife of Lycus, King of Thebes, who had divorced his former wife, Antiope. Dirce treated Antiope with great cruelty, so that when Zethus and Amphion, the sons of Antiope, obtained possession of Thebes, they took vengeance upon Dirce. They tied her to a wild bull of Mount Cithæron, which dragged her about till she perished.

Engraved in Mus. Bor. vol. xiv. tav. 5 and 6; Maffei, tav. 48; Clarac, Musée, pl. 811, No. 1952; 811 A. No. 1952.

Dimensions: Height, 12′·4″·0.

351. PALLAS.

A colossal Statue of Parian Marble. From the LOUVRE.

It was discovered 1797, in the neighbourhood of Velletri, among the ruins of an ancient villa. The name Pallas was given to Minerva from *Pallo*, Παλλω, to brandish a spear, as she was a goddess of war. Others derive the name with greater probability from *Pallax* (Παλλαξ) a very ancient Greek word, signifying a virgin. Homer uses the combined epithet PALLAS ATHÊNÊ.

Restorations: The whole right hand, and some portions of the left.

Engraved in Bouillon, vol. i. pl. 23; Cl. Cat. p. 133, No. 310; Clarac, Musée, pl. 320, No. 851. Musée Français.

Dimensions: Height, 10′·1″·1.

352. BORGHESE VASE.

Of Parian and Pentelic Marble. From the LOUVRE. Formerly in the Borghese Villa at Rome.

The two satyrs' heads originally had a curving handle over them, which the modern chisel has destroyed. The vase is otherwise quite perfect, and free from restoration.

Engraved in Bouillon, vol. i. pl. 80; Villa Borghese, St. 2, No. 9; Admiranda, tav. 50 and 51; Cl. Cat., p. 259, No. 711; Clarac, Musée, pl. 130, No. 142.

353. MEDICI VASE.

Of Marble. From the FLORENCE GALLERY.

The upper half of this vase lay many years in a storehouse belonging to the Gallery, regarded as a superior piece of sculpture, and supposed to belong to the Medici Vase, then at Rome, which consisted of the lower half only,—Zannoni, p. 262. The head of Achilles is not in the middle of the body, but nearer to the left shoulder,—Zannoni, p. 267.

Engraved in Galleria di Firenze, vol. iii. p. 156; Admiranda, Nos. 18, 19.

354. VASE (CRATÊR), WITH HEADS.

Carrara Marble. From the LOUVRE. Formerly in the Palazzo Lanti at Rome. Handles gracefully twisted.

Engraved in Clarac, Musée, pl. 145, No. 124.

355. VASE, WITH BACCHIC MASKS.

Of Parian Marble. From the LOUVRE. Formerly in the Villa Borghese at Rome.

The form of this vase shows it to be of the class of vases called *cratêr*. They were generally large, and used at entertainments for mixing the wine, which was never drank without a certain admixture of water in a fixed proportion.

The masks represent a young faun's head with pointed ears, and three of Silenus, crowned with ivy and a fir branch. Near the ivy-crowned Silenus mask lie the cymbals, and on the sides the pedum and thyrsus mark the connection between Bacchus and the fauns. The curved sides of the vase are gracefully curtained by a *nebris*, or fawn-skin, hanging by a fillet from thyrsus to thyrsus. This vase is remarkable for the beauty of its design and execution. It is fortunately in excellent condition.

Restorations : The foot, and some portions of the lip.
Engraved in Bouillon, vol. iii. Vases, pl. 9.

356. VASE (CRATÊR).

From the CAMPO SANTO, at Pisa.

With Nymphs and Bacchus, and Pan with ox-feet. Bacchus (Dionysos), Pan and the Hours.

Engraved in Lasinio, Sculture del Campo Santo, tav. 61 ; Gerhard, Ant. Bild. pl. 45, No. 3 ; compare Mus. Bor. 7, 9.

357. FOUNTAIN IN FORM OF A TRIPOD.

One block of Pentelic Marble. From the LOUVRE. Found in Hadrian's Villa at Tivoli. It formerly stood at the entrance of the Capitol at Rome.

The basin part of the tripod is fluted, and the pipe for water was conveyed through the baluster in the centre; each capital is adorned with a figure of Scylla, but no two are alike; Lion's masks project between the capitals. Caylus describes this falsely as of black marble.

Engraved in Bouillon, vol. iii., Fontaines, No. 1 ; Clarac, Musée, pl. 260, No. 647 ; Cl. Cat. No. 207 ; Mus. Cap. vol. iv. p. 370 ; Mus. Nap. No. 15. Musée Français.

358. CUPID ENCIRCLED BY DOLPHIN.

A Group in Grechetto Marble. From NAPLES. Formerly in the Farnese Collection at Rome.

Restorations : The head and feet of Cupid, by Solari ; also tail of dolphin.
Engraved in Mus. Bor. vol. ii. tav. 9 ; Clarac, Musée, pl. 646, No. 1468 ; Neapels, p. 119, No. 428.

359. AMAZON.

From the VATICAN.

360. CERES.

Little Statue. From the VATICAN.

361. MERCURY.

Sitting Bronze Figure. From HERCULANEUM.

362. MEDICI VENUS (APHRODITÊ).

363. ATHLETE.

364. POSIDONIUS.

See Portrait Gallery.

365. POLYMNIA.

Statue. From NAPLES.

366. BRONZE STATUE OF A YOUTH.

From BERLIN.

367. FAUN.

From the CAPITOL.

368. ANTINOUS AND HIS GENIUS.

A group. From MADRID.

369. DANCING FAUN.

From FLORENCE.

Presented by the Hon. E. Stanhope.

370. SLEEPING FAUN.

Upper part of figure, see statue No. 19.

371. BUST OF MELEAGER.

372. BRONZE FAUN (SATYR) SLEEPING.

Statue, life-size, of Bronze. From NAPLES. Found in Herculaneum, 1756, March 6th.

Two glands under the chin are very remarkable. Very slim boy. The action closely resembles that of the famous Barberini Faun, now at Munich, No. 19. This young faun sleeps sitting upon a mass of rock, his right arm bent over his head, and the left hanging lifelessly at his side. The two excrescences on his neck, resembling those of goats, are called by Hippocrates *Satyriasmoi* or *Phereæ*.

Dimensions : Height, 4′·3″·0.

373. APOLLO SAUROCTONOS, WITH DELICATELY MINUTE LIZARD UPON A KNOTTY TREE.

Small Bronze Statue. From the VILLA ALBANI.

Restorations : The lizard, which is exactly like a modern Roman bronze. Comp. Clarac, Musée, pl. 486A, No. 905E (see No. 258).
Dimensions : Height, 3′·1″·7.

374. SMALL SITTING FIGURE OF URANIA.

375. BRONZE STATUE OF A YOUTH.

From FLORENCE.

376. SMALL FIGURE OF CERES.

From the Vatican.

377. APOLLO LYCIUS.

From Florence.

378. THE DOG MOLOSSUS.

From Florence.

379. WRESTLERS, OR PANCRATIASTÆ.

From Florence.

380. BRONZE STATUE OF A BOY EXTRACTING A THORN.

From the Capitol, at Rome.

381. ANTONINUS PIUS.

See Portrait Gallery, No. 47.

382. INDIAN BACCHUS.

A Bronze Bust. From Herculaneum, discovered in 1759. Called, at first, Plato.

A remarkably fine bronze. The hair is long and crisp; it is bound immediately over the forehead by a band. The expression of the downcast face is somewhat melancholy. A peculiar tuft beneath the lower lip is observable, and to be seen in other statues of the Elder Bacchus also.

Engraved in Mus. Bor. vol. i. tav. 46; Bronzi d'Ercolano, vol. ii. tav. 29; Antichita d'Ercolano, vol. v. tav. 29.

383. BUST OF LAUGHING FAUN (Satyr).

Known as Fauno colla Macchia, of Parian Marble, resembling ivory in its whiteness and fineness of grain. From Munich. Formerly in the Villa Albani; said to have been found in the tomb of Cecilia Metella, in the Campagna of Rome.

The name *colla Macchia* or *à la tache* is derived from an iron tinge upon the right cheek and shoulder. One of the most beautiful and precisely modelled heads of antiquity; the entire work displays the most refined delicacy and softness of texture appropriate to youth. The ears are pointed, and the hair is short. One projection peculiar to goats is observable on the right side of the neck. The ancients called them *φηρεα*. The other projection was destroyed by some injury to the marble. On the right side of his neck appears one of the goat-like warts peculiar to the satyrisk tribe.

Engraved in Glyptothek Cat. No. 100; Bouillon, vol. i. pl. 76.

384. BUST OF ACHILLES.

Similar to No. 398, but in much worse condition.

385. DOUBLE HERMES, OR TERMINAL BUST.

Small heads, one of a laughing Faun and the other like Alexander, which is covered with skin of elephant's head, without extending over the Faun. The elephant's flat ears hang down on each side, forming a separation between the two busts.

386. BEARDED BACCHUS.

A bust crowned with vine leaves and fillets on each side. The hair of head and beard is divided into numerous distinct locks, as in several examples in the British Museum (see Vaux, p. 195).

387. BACCHUS (DIONYSOS), WINGED AND BEARDLESS.

Small Marble Bust. From the Museum of BERLIN. Found at Narni.

Restorations: The nose and bust.

Published by Dr. Emil Braun.

388. ZEUS TROPHONIOS.

A Marble Head, belonging to Prince Talleyrand; called by others Crœsus, Polycrates, and Porsenna.

Engraved in Gerhard Archäologische Zeitung, No. 1, taf. 1.

389. HEAD OF APOLLO, WITH HAIR GATHERED INTO A PECULIAR KNOT.

390. JUPITER.

Bust with drapery over left shoulder; *strophium* round head; nose remarkably long.

391. DOUBLE HERMES, OR TERMINAL BUST.

Two female heads, one with plain band like Ariadne; the other with a band of triple-plaited hair arching over head.

392. HEAD OF APOLLO.

The hair braided in an archaic manner. The eyeballs are indicated.

393. JUPITER SERAPIS.

Small bust with *modius* upon head. The hair arranged in double row of locks over forehead. The eyeballs are marked. Neck bare.

394. THE SUN (HÊLIOS).

Called the ALEXANDER of the CAPITOL. A Bust in Pentelic Marble. From the CAPITOL at Rome.

Ancient art and mythology frequently exhibit the sun with attributes different from those of Apollo. The god of day is represented with a serene and tranquil physiognomy; his floating curls are restrained partly by a band or *strophium*, in which may be seen seven holes for the insertion of bronze gilt rays or spikes. The same character of head and hair are preserved on the coins of Rhodes, which bear the head of the colossus representing the sun. Hesiod and Apollodorus, in their genealogies, both distinguish the son and daughter of Hyperion from the children of Jupiter. When Homer relates the story of Sol, or the sun, detecting the crime of Venus and Mars, he includes Apollo among the gods of Olympus to witness the strange sight afforded by Vulcan. Diana, in the same way, invariably chaste, is distinct from the Selene or Moon, who visited Endymion upon Mount Latmos, and was known also for other attachments of the same kind.

Engraved in Bouillon, vol. i. pl. 75; Mus. Nap. 189.

395. JUNO.

With large plain *sphendone*, or frontlet. Hard in execution, and very much distorted.

396. APOLLO.

Head of a Statue. From the Cabinet of Count Pourtalès-Gorgier, at PARIS. Formerly in the Giustiniani Collection at Rome.

The exuberance of hair is quite extraordinary; the style and arrangement of it remind us, notwithstanding, of the Belvedere Apollo. There is an expression of pain in the countenance, which does not accord with other representations of the divinity.

Engraved in Antiques du Cabinet Pourtalès, pl. 14; and in Oesterley, Part ii. taf. 11, No. 123.

397. HEAD OF THE LAOCOON.

From the Gallery of the Duke d'Aremberg, at BRUSSELS.

Although evidently a repetition of the head of the celebrated Laocoon found near the Palace of Titus, it displays several essential differences in respect to style of art. The entire forms seem more softened—melted down, if the expression may be permitted—the hair rounder and less picturesque than in the Vatican statue, and the eyeballs marked, which cannot be traced in the Vatican figure. The mouth is wider and more open, strongly displaying the teeth. The expression in this head is vehement and agonised, imparting a feeling of pain to the beholder which no work of art should do. The Vatican head exhibits the teeth also, but with less distortion of the mouth. An opinion was circulated in the French papers about February, 1841, that this was the original head of the Vatican figure. The story ran, that when the group was first discovered the head was *wanting*, and that one had been supplied by a practised sculptor from an antique *bas-relief*. Subsequently the original was found by some Venetians, who sold it to the father of the Prince for 160,000*l.*; and the story proceeds to say that Napoleon offered the Duke its weight in gold for it. See No. 16 for account of the original and its restorations. This head is most probably a modern work.

398. ACHILLES.

Bust of Parian Marble. From MUNICH. Formerly in the Villa Albani, at Rome.

Named in the numerous repetitions in other collections either Mars or Achilles. (Compare statue No. 310.) The helmet has a sphinx instead of crest, and a griffin on either side; the frontlet is ornamented with two dogs, having a palmette between them. The whiskers are strongly marked, and the bust altogether is a repetition of No. 384. It is a fine work of Grecian art.

Restorations : The crest and sphinx.
Engraved in Piroli, Mus. Nap. ii. 59 ; Glyptothek, No. 83.

399. ÆSCULAPIUS (Asklêpios).

Bust of Parian Marble.

The head is characterized by a kind of turban or twisted band, called theristrion (θεριστριον), peculiar to this god. The countenance displays considerable resemblance to Jupiter. This is a portion of an entire statue attributable to the best period of Grecian art. The figure is continued considerably below the chest. The body is bare.

Engraved in Bouillon, vol. i. pl. 71 ; Mus. Nap. No. 14.

400. FEMALE BUST.

The fragment of a Statue. From the Arundel Collection, at Oxford.

The drapery covering one breast. The largeness of the forms and the treatment of the marble show a decided affinity to the sculptures of the time of Phidias, which Mr. Newton was the first to point out.

The nose has been very badly restored.
Described by Dr. Waagen, Treasures of Art, vol. iii. p. 52.

401. PHILOSOPHER.

Very small Bust.

402. BUST OF DRAPED FEMALE.

403. PLUTO.

404. OMPHALE.

A Bust of Pentelic Marble. From the Louvre. Formerly in the Villa Albani where it was called Iole.

A very superior work of art.

Restorations : All except the mask.
Engraved in Bouillon, vol. ii. pl. 67 ; Cl. Cat. No. 193, p. 88.

405. BUST OF ARIADNE, or ARETHUSA.

A band passes across the forehead.

406. SERAPIS, or INFERNAL JUPITER.

Head set on to another bust, which is naked, with the exception of a mantle, fastened by a clasp or *fibula* on the right shoulder.

407. PARIS.

Bust of Pentelic Marble. From the Villa Albani.

The lover of Helen is dressed in the Phrygian cap, his beautiful hair in curls more like a woman's style ; for this his noble brother Hector reproaches him in the Iliad.

408. BUST OF MINERVA MEDICA.

See statue No. 18.

409. BUST OF PALLAS.

410. MEDUSA.

From the Glyptothek, at Munich. Formerly in the collection of the Marquis Rondanini at Rome.

This mask has suggested to our illustrious Flaxman the *Gorgon* expression in some of his outline illustrations to Æschylus.

Restorations: The tip of the nose and one of the nostrils; part of the hair; and the side portions of the serpents.

Engraved in Guattani, Monumenti inediti, 1788; Aprile, tav. 2. p. xxxiv.; Glyptothek Catalogue, No. 132.

411. BUST OF REPOSING FAUN.

See statue No. 12.

412. HEAD OF A CHILD.

Crowned with ivy leaves and berries. At the back of the head, where the hair is sometimes gathered in a knot, is a small ox-head and horns.

413. JUPITER.

Small Bust.

414. Part of a SEPULCHRAL ALTAR.

Of Marble. From the Vatican. Found on the Esquiline hill, and formerly in the Villa Negroni.

This remarkably shaped monument is supported by four feet made out of the same piece with the rest; it is highly decorated on the four sides with architectural ornaments. The bas-relief on the principal front represents the Visit of Bacchus to Icarius—a subject often repeated in ancient art. Repetitions will be found in the British Museum and the Louvre. Icarius, with his daughter Erigone, on the couch, welcome their divine visitor, who appears as a corpulent person with flowing beard. A young satyr takes off his shoes, and another supports him. His attendants follow,—two fauns, and Silenus, who plays the double flutes; an old man supports a female; and the scene is terminated by a phallic figure upon a pedestal. A curtain is extended behind the principal personages. At the back of this pedestal are two centaurs with smaller figures upon them, and between the centaurs are two cupids, each holding a butterfly over a candelabrum and two burning torches. The sides are ornamented with pastoral subjects. On one, a man milking a goat, a tree, and female statue behind him; a young woman is caressing the goat. On the other side, a doe and its young, observed by a girl and youth: a standing figure of Hercules on pedestal to the right. This monument is now in the Braccio Nuovo, and serves as a pedestal for a small group of the Graces.

Engraved in Mus. Pio. Clem. vol. iv. tav. 25; compare Admiranda, tav. 43; Terra-cottas of British Museum, No. 47; Vaux's Handbook, p. 241. Bunsen, vol. ii. part 2, pages 97 and 98.

415. OMPHALE.

Bust, with lion's skin covering head. The legs of the skin tied over breast. Very poor work, probably cinque cento.

416. STAG REARING, WITH A DOG ON ITS BACK.

694 R., E. B. From the Sala Degli Animali, in the VATICAN. The greater part modern.

Engraved in Pistolesi, vol. v. tav. 15 ; Bunsen, vol. ii. part 2, page 162.

417. ROEBUCK STANDING, WITH DOG ON ITS BACK.

Small-sized Group. From the VATICAN, in the Sala degli Animali.

Engraved in Pistolesi, vol. v. tav. 4 ; Bunsen, vol. ii. part 2, p. 162.

418. NYMPH.

A small Statue of Greek Marble. From the LOUVRE. Formerly in the Borghese Villa.

Probably the figure was an astragal player, but has been converted into "La Venus à la Coquille." The fine and delicate drapery reminds the spectator of the little statue (20 R.) for similar treatment. The right shoulder and both arms are modern restorations. A similar figure in the British Museum, Ancient Marbles, part 2, pl. 28.

Engraved in Bouillon, pl. 15 ; Villa Borghese, st. 4, No. 11.
Dimensions: Height, 1′·10″·0.

419. NYMPH AT FOUNTAIN.

From the BRITISH MUSEUM.

420. SMALL STATUE OF SITTING HERCULES.

421. CATO AND PORCIA.

Half-figures from a Roman Tomb. Of Luni Marble, life-size. From the VATICAN.

Purchased by Clement XIV., in 1770, from the Villa Mattei. These figures are excellent portraits of a Roman and his wife together, as often seen upon Roman tombs ; they belong to the time of Augustus, conjecturing from the arrangement of the lady's hair.

Engraved in Visconti, Mus. Pio Clem. vol. vii. tav. 25 ; Pistolesi, vol. v. tav. 47 ; Bunsen, vol. ii. part 2, p. 187 ; Mus. Nap. No. 125 ; Musée Royal, vol. 2.

422. BRONZE PLATES FROM ETRUSCAN CHARIOT.

From MUNICH.

These plates formed part of an Etruscan chariot discovered at Perugia in 1812 ; it was probably coated on both sides with bronze. They were found in fragments ; some portion went to the Museum at Perugia ; the greater part was acquired by Mr. Dodwell, from whom they passed into the hands of the King of Bavaria.

A. Originally formed of two parts, but found united ; to the left a boar-hunt, a man with dog in a leash, followed by a sea monster or hippocamp. Next to this, turning away to the right, is a floating female, with four wings or fins, she is dressed in a long garment, like the dresses seen in the sculptures from Nineveh (Layard, pl. 33 of MONUMENTS OF NINEVEH, 1st series, 1849); an archer precedes the winged female.

B. A gorgon seizing two lions ; a hippocamp and long-necked bird in the spaces to the right. The style remarkably like that seen on the metal work, recently brought home by Mr. Layard.

C. Minotaur.

D. Female figure, called Spes (Elpis), holding her garment with the left hand, and a flask in her right.

Engraved in Inghirami, Mon. Etruschi, Serie 3, tav. 23 ; Glyptothek Catalogue, Nos. 32—38.

423. ÆSOP STATUE.

From VILLA ALBANI.

Engraved in Bunsen, vol. iii. part 2, page 541 ; Visconti, Icon. Grecque, vol. i. Pl. 11. No. 12.

See Portrait Gallery, No. 3.

NOT YET ARRIVED.

219. MODEL OF THE COLISEUM AT ROME.

220. MODEL OF THE TRAJAN COLUMN AT ROME.

ADORANTE, RESTORÉE EN EUTERPE.

Statue, large life, of Greek Parian Marble. From the LOUVRE. Formerly in the Borghese Collection.

Restorations: Feet, arms, attributes, nose, lips, chin, and portions of drapery.

Engraved in Bouillon, pl. 44 ; Villa Borghese, St. i., No. 8 ; Cl. Cat., No. 299, p. 129.

ADORANTE, WITH OPEN HANDS.

Statue, life-size. From the LOUVRE. Formerly in the Borghese Collection at ROME.

Engraved in Bouillon, vol. ii. pl. 29 ; Villa Borghese ; Cl. Cat.

ÆNEAS.

A Bust of Pentelic Marble. From the LOUVRE. Formerly in the Villa Borghese.

The head does not belong to the bust : it is of different marble ; but both are of excellent workmanship. The back of the head and helmet is modern.

The hero looks upwards with an agonized expression. The helmet is very low, and scarcely perceptible from the front. The hair starts all round from the face and cheeks.

Engraved in Bouillon, vol. ii. pl. 68.

ÆSCULAPIUS (Asklêpios).

Statue of Pentelic Marble, heroic size. Formerly in the Villa Albani, at Rome.

This specimen is much injured by extensive and ill-executed restorations; the form of the thighs and knee-caps seen through the drapery has been almost entirely destroyed. The right fore-arm and left leg are of modern and clumsy work. The back part of the serpent is all that is antique. The head of Æsculapius is well preserved, and perfect, with the exception of the nose.

Engraved in Bouillon, vol. i. pl. 48; Millin, Gal. Myth. No. 99, pl. 31; Annales du Musée, vol. vi. pl. 54.

ARIADNE.

Bust of the Capitol, of Pentelic Marble.

The beloved of Bacchus is seen here in all her beauty; her forehead is encircled with a Bacchic diadem; her tresses, interwoven with the leaves of ivy, are gathered into a knot behind, escaping from which, they fall joyously over the neck. Winckelmann especially admired the graceful contour of the eyes and cheeks.

Restorations: The tip of the nose, also the greater part of the breast. The lower lip, and part of the upper; they have been very badly executed.

Engraved in Bouillon, vol. i. pl. 74; Winckelmann, Mon. Ined. No. 55; Bunsen, vol. iii. part 1, p. 255; Mus. Nap. No. 150.

BAS-RELIEF OF A COMIC SCENE.

BAS-RELIEF—Horses.

Two horses in basso-rilievo, in good action, but rather hard style. The part to the left, containing a chariot, is wanting, but a left hand of the driver remains. The hardness of workmanship, together with the great spirit of the animals, remind one of the celebrity that Calamis obtained for representing horses, accompanied by the remark of Quintilian that there was a certain hardness about the works of this artist.

Restorations: The right hoofs, before and behind, and front knee.

Engraved in Gall. di Fir. vol. ii. tav. 86.

BOY AND GOOSE.

Of Pentelic Marble. From the Louvre. Found at Roma Vecchia, the site of the ancient Pagus Lemonius. Compare 269.

Engraved in Cl. Cat. No. 694; Clarac. Musée, pl. 293, No. 2226.

BUST OF SCIPIO AFRICANUS.

Found at Herculaneum, in the villa of the Papyri.

Engraved in H. B. South, p. 177.

CENTAUR BORGHESE.

Found on the Cælian Hill at ROME. (S. Bartoli Memorie. No. 51.)

Engraved in Villa Borghese, St. 9, No. 1; Bouillon, vol. i. pl. 64; Clarac, Musée, pl. 277, No. 1782; Cl. Cat. No. 134.

CERES (DÊMÊTÊR).

A Colossal Statue of Pentelic Marble. From the VATICAN. Found among the ruins of the Theatre of Pompey at Rome.

Restorations: The two arms, the right foot, and four toes of the left foot. *Engraved in* Bouillon, pl. 3; Mus. Pio Clem. vol. ii. pl. 27; Pistolesi, vol. v. tav. 105.

CROUCHING VENUS (APHRODITÊ).

Similar in action to the Vatican one: a bracelet on right arm. Venus accroupie.

Engraved in Bouillon, vol. iii. pl. 6, No. 6; Cl. Cat. No. 681; Clarac, Musée, pl. 345, No. 1416.

DOMITIAN.

Colossal Bust. From VILLA ALBANI.

Engraved in Mus. Nap., No. 13.

EUTERPE.

Life-size. From BERLIN.

A beautiful portrait of a Roman lady, with crimped hair. Very similar to one of the daughters of Balbus, found at Herculaneum.

Engraved in Mus. Bor. vol. ii. t. 41.

FLORA (CHLORIS).

Colossal Statue of Grechetto Marble. From NAPLES. Formerly in the Farnese Palace at Rome. Found in the Baths of Caracalla, together with the Farnese Hercules. Commonly called the FARNESE FLORA.

Visconti would infer, from the action of raising the garment, that the original character of the figure was the goddess Spes (Elpis.) Della Porta first made it into a Flora (Mus. Bor. text, p. 2). The head, arms, and legs were first restored by Giacomo della Porta, and afterwards by Albaccini and Tagliolini, but without any authority.

Engraved in Mus. Bor. vol. ii. tav. 26; Maffei, tav. 51; Clarac, Musée, pl. 438, No. 795 D.; No. 200 of Naples Catalogue; Neapels, p. 63, No. 200.

FLORENCE HERMAPHRODITE.

Recumbent Statue of Parian Marble. From the UFFIZII at FLORENCE. Transferred by the Grand Duke Frederick II. from the Villa Ludovisi.

The difference in the present appearance of this statue from the Borghese and Louvre ones consists in the absence of drapery upon the legs.

Restorations: The right leg and thigh, and half the nates, the left leg, and half the thigh, and part of the bed on that side.

Engraved in Museum Florentinum, tav. 40; Gall. di Firenze, vol. ii. tav. 58; Clarac, Musée, pl. 668, No. 1547; Wicar, Gal. de Florence, vol. i.

HERCULES (HÊRAKLÊS).

Bust of Pentelic Marble. From the VILLA ALBANI.

Wrought with wonderful facility and general effect. Hercules is crowned and adorned with broad fillets, which hang on each side of his neck. He is represented here as a victor in the Olympian games.

Restorations: The tip of the nose.

Engraved in Bouillon, vol. i. pl. 75.

HERMAPHRODITE.

With drapery on right leg, and toe entangled.

Engraved in Bouillon, vol. iii. pl. 14; Maffei, tav. 78.

HERMAPHRODITE.

Statue, less than life, of Pentelic Marble. From the LOUVRE. Formerly in the Borghese Collection.

Many repetitions of this statue exist in other galleries. The mattress is antique, and very little of the figure betrays restoration. An imitation of No. , in the Louvre also. A peculiarity of this figure consists in the bed being less level than in the Louvre or Florence statues. It affords a more graceful pose for the figure. The ground slopes down considerably to the left side of the figure, and displays the long-drawn folds passing from the body across the arm to great advantage.

Restorations: The entire right arm, a great part of the face, neck, and portions of the body and thighs, and half the legs, but executed in the most skilful manner.

Engraved in Clarac, Cat. No. 461, p. 184; Bouillon, vol. iii. pl. 14; Villa Borghese.

INDIAN BACCHUS.

Colossal Bust of Pentelic Marble. From the LOUVRE. Formerly in the Villa Borghese.

This bust is treated in a grand manner, and is fortunately well preserved. The mouth and eyes deserve especial attention for their beauty of form and truth to nature. The drapery is modern. The hair is carefully parted in the middle, and arranged in long metallic lines; a narrow cord encircles the head. Immediately beneath the lower lip distinct series of small curls appears.

Engraved in Bouillon, vol. i. pl. 72.

INDIAN BACCHUS.

Bust of dark Rosso-antico Marble. Found at ROME in 1791, between the Cælian and Esquiline hills, in the quarter called Merulana.

Bacchus, the conqueror of the East, wearing a long beard, and having his hair arranged in long tresses entwined with a band. The eyes were hollowed to receive enamel or precious stones. The oldest representations of Bacchus were always bearded. He was represented as a serious majestic old man, with luxurious hair, encircled with a band, holding the wine-cup and vine-branch in his hands. His dress was long and full, almost effeminate. This accords with the description of the deity given by Pausanias as represented on that primitive work, the Chest of Cypselus. On the early stage also, he wore the long robe, and over that again the *peplos* or mantle, woven by the Graces. Thus he invariably appears on the ancient painted vases, many of which may be seen in the British Museum. The *nebris*, or fawn-skin, became an early attribute of the god. It was not until the age of Praxiteles that Bacchus acquired the slender youthful form in which an effeminate character prevailed. No covering then remained, with the exception of the *nebris;* but in all the more sacred representations, the robe and beard seem never to have been set aside. We may therefore regard what is called the Indian Bacchus as the Elder Bacchus.

Engraved in Mus. Nap. No. 43.

INDIAN BACCHUS (Dionysos).

Statue of Pentelic Marble. From the Vatican.

Discovered in 1761, near Frascati, six miles from Rome, in a place called Prata Porzia,—the remains of a villa of Lucius Verus. It stood in a niche with four Caryatides, now in the Villa Albani. The border of the mantle across the breast is inscribed,

CAPΔANAΠAΛΛOC

See an interesting note upon the false inscriptions among the ancients themselves, in the text description of Bouillon's pl. 28. The Caryatides are of very inferior execution. Cavaceppi says, "Trovato in una vigna vicino Frascati in luogo chiamato Pietra Portia, presso di me."

Restorations: The tip of the nose, the lips, and entire right arm. It probably held a thyrsus.

Engraved in Mus. Pio Clem. vol. ii. tav. 41; Bouillon, vol. i. pl. 28; Bunsen, vol. ii. p. 239; Maffei; Pistolesi, vol. vi. tav. 7; Clarac, Musée, pl. 684, No. 1602; Winckelmann, Mon. Ined. No. 163; Cavaceppi, vol. iii. No. 27; Mus. Nap. No. 140; Musée Français.

ISIS.

A Bust of Black Marble. From the Louvre. Formerly in the Villa Borghese.

The head is covered with a short veil, which terminates in fringe upon the shoulders. An owl is carved on the support, which is indeed of the same piece with the bust. This bust is remarkable for its complete preservation; it is intact.

Engraved in Bouillon, vol. i. pl. 77.

ISIS.

A Bust. From the Vatican.

JUNO.

Statue colossal, 7.2 of Pentelic Marble. From Berlin.

No. 14, Berlin Catalogue.

JUNO (Hêrê) OF THE CAPITOL.

Statue, heroic, of Parian Marble. From the Capitol at Rome. Formerly in the Palazzo Cesi, where it was called an Amazon.

The left arm with hand upon hip most probably modern, as Maffei represents it covered with drapery. Of grand style and effectively treated. The head is certainly antique, but does not seem to have originally belonged to the figure.

Engraved in Bouillon, pl. 2 ; Mus. Cap. vol. iii. tav. 8 ; Maffei, tav. 129 ; Bunsen, p. 253 (vol. 1-3) ; Mori, vol. ii., Sala Grande, tav. 17 ; Mus. Nap. No. 147.

JUPITER SERAPIS—Bust with Modius and no Rays.

Of Parian Marble, without tunic ; the breast is bare, but drapery covers his left shoulder.

The mask and beard are all that is antique ; the rest is the caprice of the modern artist. The physiognomy is more in accordance with the Jupiter Olympius, whose divine majesty is far above that of Serapis.

Restorations : The hair of the head, and modius and chest also.
Engraved in Bouillon, vol. i. pl. 71.

LA PROVIDENCE.

Statue, heroic, of Pentelic Marble. From the Louvre.

Engraved in Cl. Cat. p. 137, No. 323 ; Clarac, Musée, pl. 330, No. 1896.

MENELAUS BUST.

Of Pentelic Marble. Found, together with many fragments, by Gavin Hamilton, in Hadrian's Villa, at Tivoli, at a spot called Pantanello.

This head belonged originally to a group of Menelaus, carrying away the body of Patroclus, who had been slain by Hector. The action is very expressive. Menelaus, the King of Sparta, seems to be calling upon the Greeks to aid in securing the body of the hero he is supporting, which he desires to deliver to his friend Achilles. The helmet is adorned with the combat of Hercules with the Centaurs, and the visor with two gryphons, which the ignorance of the restorers has changed into eagles. Three groups of antique workmanship representing this subject are extant. Two at Florence are in the Pitti Palace, the other upon the Ponte Vecchio, and the third at Rome, under the name of Pasquino, which is considered by judges to be one of the finest statues in that city (see Bunsen, vol. iii. part 3, p. 399 ; Maffei, No. 42). To judge from the execution, although the surface has been much corroded by time, the statue was only a copy of a much superior work.

Restorations : The nose, lips, part of the left cheek, the entire bust, and part of neck.

Engraved in Mus. Pio Clem. vol. vi. pl. 18 and 19 ; Mus. Nap. No. 215; Bouillon, vol. ii. pl. 68.

MINERVA BUST.

Pentelic Marble. Found in the neighbourhood of the Mausoleum of Hadrian, at Rome. It was for many years in the Castle of St. Angelo until removed to the Vatican by Pius VI.

The goddess is armed with her helmet and ægis. The ram's heads upon the former may be allusive to the engine of war which bears the same shape and name.

Engraved in Mus. Nap. No. 178.

MUSE.

Restored as one of the daughters of Lycomedes. From BERLIN.

Engraved in Clarac, Musée, pl. 537, No. 1129.

NEBRID BACCHUS (DIONYSOS).

Heroic Statue of Pentelic Marble. From the LOUVRE. Brought from the Garden at Versailles. Called sometimes the NEBRID BACCHUS.

Filleted and crowned with ivy-leaves and clusters. The *nebris*, or fawn-skin, is the only covering to his body, and lies very close upon the skin. Few antique specimens have been better preserved. No restorations marked in Clarac.

Restorations: The tips of fingers to both hands.

Engraved in Bouillon, vol. i. pl. 30; Cl. Cat. p. 70, No. 148; Clarac, Musée, pl. 275, No. 1574; Mus. Nap. No. 144.

NIOBÊ SARCOPHAGUS.

From the Galleria dei Candelabri, in the VATICAN.

PÆTUS AND ARRIA.

From the VILLA LUDOVISI. Found most probably together with the Dying Gladiator in the gardens of Sallust. Called by Clarac, MACAREUS and CANACE.

The head of the man clearly characterises a barbarian. Very probably this group, as well as the Dying Gladiator, decorated some monument to commemorate a victory over barbarians.

Engraved in Clarac, Musée, pl. 825, No. 2072; Bunsen, vol. iii. part 2, p. 587.

PALÆMON.

A Bust of Pentelic Marble.

Very delicate feminine face, with a peculiar head-dress, like a skin tied over the head, and bound by a band on the forehead: at each side remain tenons of iron, by which additional pieces, perhaps, of fins, were originally attached. Visconti was the first to call the statue Palæmon, a marine god worshipped by the Romans as Portumnus.

Engraved in Bouillon, vol. i. pl. 76.

PROVIDENTIA—PROVIDENCE.

Statue, life-size, of Pentelic Marble, the head of Grecco Marble. From the LOUVRE. Formerly in the Château Richelieu.

A majestic standing figure, holding a globe, *stephane* on head; in fact a Urania. The tip of the nose and both the arms and feet are modern. Similar figures are seen on Roman imperial coins, inscribed Providentia.

Engraved in Bouillon, pl. 60; Cl. Cat. No. 323, p. 138.

ROME.

Bust of Carrara Marble. From the LOUVRE. Formerly in the Villa Borghese.

In a low helmet, with crest, and two animals on the sides; clothed in tunic, *pallium* over her left shoulder. The lower eyelids are marked to indicate eyelashes.

Engraved in Bouillon, vol. i. pl. 78.

ROME.

A Bust.

SALPION VASE.

From NAPLES. Found at Formiæ, and removed to Gaeta, where it served as the Cathedral font.

Engraved in H. B. p. 167.

SIBYL.

Statue of Greek Marble. From NAPLES. FARNESE.

Portrait of a Roman Lady, with pallium thrown over head; hair arranged peculiarly: she holds a roll in left hand.

THE TRIUMPH OF TITUS, WITH THE JEWISH SPOILS.

Alto-Relievo, from the Arch of Titus.

THE MOST CELEBRATED BERNINI HERMAPHRODITE.

Recumbent Statue of Luni Marble. From the LOUVRE. Formerly in the Borghese Collection at Rome.

The mattress sculptured by Bernini. A repetition is in the Louvre, and another at Florence. Two others still remain in the Palazza Borghese, at Rome.

Engraved in Bouillon, pl. 63; Maffei, tav. 78; Villa Borghese, st. 6, No. 7; Cl. Cat. p. 205, No. 527; Clarac, Musée, pl. 303, No. 1552.

TIBERIUS, IN THE TOGA.

From the LOUVRE.

Engraved in Bouillon, vol. ii. pl. 34; Cl. Cat. p. 53, No. 111; Clarac, Musée, pl. 336, No. 2357.

TRIANGULAR ALTAR OF THE TWELVE GODS.

From the LOUVRE.

VASE OF THE CAPITOL.

Engraved in Mus. Capit. vol. iv. tav. 21; Mori, vol. ii.; Stanza del Vaso, tav. 1.

VENUS OF CNIDOS.

From the GLYPTOTHEK, at MUNICH.

The Venus was still at Cnidos during the reign of the Emperor Arcadius, about four hundred years after Christ. This statue seems to offer the first idea of the Venus de' Medici, which is likely to be the repetition of another Venus, also the work of this artist, mentioned by Pliny (Flaxman, p. 91).

Engraved in Clarac, Musée, pl. 618, No. 1377; Flaxman, pl. 22.

WOUNDED AMAZON, BY CTESILAS.

Restored in long robe. RICHELIEU.

With drapery round the neck, and from the same original as the Richelieu, in Clarac, Musée, pl. 811, No. 2036.

Engraved in Cl. Cat. p. 122, No. 281; Comp. Mori, vol. ii. Sala Grande, tav. 21; Clarac, Musée, pl. 265, No. 2033; the Capitol one, Clarac, Musée, pl. 812B, No. 2032; Bunsen, vol. iii. pl. 232.

YOUNG HERCULES (HÊRAKLÊS).

A Bust of Parian Marble. From the LOUVRE. Formerly in Château Richelieu.

The face is beardless; part of a skin hangs over the back of the neck and down the left side. The hair starts up in short curls all round forehead. A band encircles the head.

Restorations: The nose, ears and mouth, which have been very inexpertly supplied.

Engraved in Bouillon, vol. ii. pl. 67.

BRADBURY AND EVANS, PRINTERS, WHITEFRIARS.

1373864R0

Printed in Great Britain by
Amazon.co.uk, Ltd.,
Marston Gate.